HALF WILD

HALF WILD

People, Dogs, and Environmental Policy

Dave Dempsey

Illustrations by Logan Hudson

MICHIGAN STATE UNIVERSITY PRESS | *East Lansing*

♾ The paper used in this publication meets the minimum requirements of
ANSI/NISO Z39.48-1992 (R 1997) (Permanence of Paper).

Michigan State University Press
East Lansing, Michigan 48823-5245

LIBRARY OF CONGRESS CATALOGING-IN-PUBLICATION DATA
Names: Dempsey, Dave, 1957– author. | Hudson, Logan, illustrator.
Title: Half wild : people, dogs, and environmental policy /
Dave Dempsey ; Illustrations by Logan Hudson.
Description: East Lansing : Michigan State University Press, [2022]
Identifiers: LCCN 2021062351 | ISBN 9781611864434 (paperback) | ISBN 9781609177133 |
ISBN 9781628954814 | ISBN 9781628964752
Subjects: LCSH: Dempsey, Dave, 1957– | Environmentalists—United States—Biography. |
Environmental policy—United States. | Environmental protection—United States. |
Climatic changes—United States.
Classification: LCC GE56.D46 A3 2022 | DDC 333.72092 [B]—dc23/eng20220314
LC record available at https://lccn.loc.gov/2021062351

Cover design by Erin Kirk
Cover art is by incomible (Adobe Stock)

Visit Michigan State University Press at www.msupress.org

Contents

To Lana Pollack
Courageous Leader, Distinguished Public Servant,
Mentor to Many, Cherished Friend

Preface

On our nightly walk in the nature reserve out back in May 2020, my little dog Fitz and I tangled. It was the second time in four days that he snapped up something on the ground before I knew what it was and could stop him. After the first infraction, he awoke in the middle of the night and vomited four times. I'll remember the evening for a while because when I took him outside at 3 a.m. to complete the job of emptying his stomach, I looked up over the parking lot to see the waning moon, Jupiter, and Saturn in a row, with Mars roughly aligned off to the east.

If I could have made Fitz understand English that night, I would have told him that my grab for whatever repellent thing was in his mouth was an attempt to protect his health and comfort. But he knew only a few words of English and probably wasn't in a mood to hear my reassurances. Instead, as I made a stab at the end of the soft black substance that dangled from his jaws, he went full Cujo. Stephen King would have drawn inspiration from the demonic snarl, the maniacal baring of the teeth. He was not going to give up his trophy without a nasty fight.

Yes, I should have trained him out of this during his puppyhood. It's one of several ways in which his upbringing fell short of an Ivy League education. At 8 p.m. that day, I could do nothing about that. I reached for his prey several times, inspiring the same bestial defense. Frustrated, I refrained from cursing him as I have before. Instead, I led him a few strides before suddenly reaching again. This was the showdown. He snapped viciously as I somehow managed to tear the whole disgusting thing from his mouth and flung it far off among the trees. The price was not high, but there was a price: he pierced my left thumb just below the nail, drawing a little blood. I've given more serum in the past for lesser causes.

He got no reprimand from me in part because he hasn't made the connection previously and because, on reflection, I believe Fitz is only doing what generations of his ancestors have done. Their biological imperative is to survive, so wild-caught game is at a premium. Sharing does not come naturally. This typically loving dog was reminding me that he does not come from millennia of pet predecessors. Something of the wild persists across all the centuries of hunting and the more recent era of plentiful free treats.

The longer I live, and the more dogs I know, the more convinced I am that canines and humans live in a half-wild world. Governed by instincts, yet civilized so that we can live together within and across species, humans and dogs straddle a boundary. This life on the border creates a tension that leads to magnificent creation and appalling destruction.

As an environmentalist nearing the end of a forty-year career trying to defend and expand the range of protection, I look back and see that I've been stepping back and forth over that boundary from the beginning. Rational, attuned to logic and reason, as I pursued the work. Impassioned, often enraged at frequent defeats; ready to damn the political process and half the human race.

"To be whole. To be complete. Wildness reminds us what it means to be human, what we are connected to rather than what we are separate from," says author and environmental defender Terry Tempest Williams. But how does being human remind us of what it means to be wild?

I'm hoping that by telling some of my stories from four decades of environmental policy work, I can see the boundary better—and help the reader become familiar with it—as if it were on a map. I hope that doing so might send out a ripple or two that reaches others, who can carry on and perhaps protect more of our precious half wild, on the Earth and in us.

Dumpsite

I n 1968, when I was eleven, my family traveled by station wagon from Dearborn, a suburb of Detroit, to Houghton, where my grandfather lived. To those who think of Michigan as two compact peninsulas, I respond that the journey consumed two days and 550 miles. That's roughly the equivalent of a drive from the Detroit area to Washington, DC.

As I remember it, my two brothers and I took turns sitting on a rear-facing deployable seat in the back of a station wagon. It was a perch in which on every trip, it seemed, one of us got motion sickness, causing a roadside stop while the victim got nauseous in the weeds.

The flipping stomachs were worth it. By the time we arrived in Houghton, we had become happily acclimated to a new way of being. Although still in the station wagon, we were moving among thick roadside forests and passing small, shining lakes. And at a few points along the way, the road suddenly emerged onto the shoreline of Lake Superior, taking my breath away. Its majesty was self-apparent.

Grandpa had been born and raised in Calumet, just north of Houghton. In his youth, the first two decades of the twentieth century, Calumet was a thriving town with an ornate opera house and more than 20,000 residents. Copper mines had attracted thousands of immigrant workers. Finland was the largest source. So many immigrants flocked to the Copper Country that one writer termed it "an interior Ellis Island."[*]

My grandmother had Finnish roots, but Grandpa descended primarily from Scots. He told us colorful stories of growing up in Calumet. I remember the macabre stories first—or did I imagine them later? Like the townsman who disappeared in mid-winter, leading some to speculate he'd run off to a chance at a better life—only to be revealed when the thick snow cover melted, a smile on his face. If I recall correctly, his last stop had been a bar.

Another story concerned a New Year's Eve celebration. At midnight, as the new year arrived, a lodger stuck his head out the second-story window to take in the fresh air of a new beginning. Unfortunately, the resident below liked to shoot his rifle into the sky to mark the change of years.

Grandpa had enlisted in World War I, served as an electrician and reached France, returning to settle in the Detroit area, where he married my grandmother. In 1968, not long after being mugged on a street near his Detroit apartment, Grandpa returned to the scenery of his youth.

Few childhood joys rivaled the expectation of seeing Grandpa. He doted on us. When babysitting, he read poetry to my brothers and me at bedtime. *The Barefoot Boy* by John Greenleaf Whittier was one of his favorites. He taught us about baseball and cracked simple jokes. He was unfailingly kind and unconditionally loving. He gave us his best.

Thinking of amusements to enjoy with my grandfather on our 1968 trip, we somehow settled on the Copper Harbor town dump. I'm not sure whose idea it was, but it makes sense that it would have been Grandpa's.

This was not just any dump. This was an open dump, its trash exposed to the elements. This was a buffet for bears.

More than half a century afterward, I can't recall how the discussion proceeded, but I must have become very excited. Bears had not rambled through my home city of Dearborn in one hundred years. All I knew about bears until then came from children's TV shows and cartoons like *Yogi Bear*. I thought they were adorable, but I also sensed a terrible power in them.

My father took photos of the scene. Perhaps a half dozen cars parked at the fringe of the dump. Piles of rotting trash and refuse in dumpsters lay beckoning for

---

[*]   Michigan Technological University, "Michigan's Copper Country: an Interior Ellis Island," https://ethnicity.lib.mtu.edu/.

the bears. Three or four feasted, seemingly unaware—but surely very aware—of the gawking tourists. The bears' performance was authentic and unrehearsed. They smelled easy food, and they capitalized on it.

As I remember that evening at the ursine tourist trap now, I feel compassion for the black bears pawing through leftover food and household hazardous waste. We should respect the dignity and the integrity of all animals, whether we favor hunting or not. The bears may have been enjoying the easy pickings, but humans were mocking them by treating them as antic action figures.

Still, in a part of the state low on year-round residents, where winter is a cruel and seemingly unending punishment, where poverty is endured stoically, the chance for a few bucks from a self-sustaining, low-overhead draw was irresistible. Like many others, we brought back memories and photos, marveling at the amazing black bears.

The Copper Harbor dump won national notoriety seven years later. The controversial CBS-TV documentary *The Guns of Autumn*, broadcast in September 1975, opened with a scene from Copper Harbor that enraged hunters across the nation. The hungry bears arrived at the peaceful dump not knowing it was the first day of firearm season. As one outdoor writer put it, what followed "was as bloody a massacre as any sportsman could conjure up in even the most dreadful of nightmares."

> CBS cameras zoomed in close as hunters slit the dead animals open, dragging intestines out onto the ground, and then tossed the limp bodies of the dead bears onto the tailgates, hoods and roofs of various types of vehicles.
>
> For several unbelievably intense moments, the blood flowed freely. One bear, only wounded by the first bullet, thrashed wildly on the forest floor before being relieved of its pain by a second shot to the head.[†]

The documentary was so controversial that most advertisers pulled their commercials before the program aired. CBS also broadcast a follow up show that allowed hunters and hunting organizations to vent. They may have had a point that the show had overall sensationally revealed an anti-hunting bias, but hunting over bait (and garbage with food waste is bait) is not hunting. It's target practice.

Other coverage of the dump was lighthearted. In 1982, after passage of a strict new solid waste law, the Associated Press reported that "the free ride may be over

---

† Reeves Feild, "Did the *Guns of Autumn* Aim Directly at Hunting?," *Shreveport Times* (LA), September 14, 1975.

for some hungry bears that feed regularly at an Upper Peninsula garbage dump." But township supervisor Don Olson rejected the idea. "You can hardly get in at the bear-feeding station. It's usually full of tourists."[‡]

A reporter for the *Detroit Free Press* described the scene in 1986:

> A woman, toting a green plastic bag of garbage, rushed through the assembly of some 50 people and a half dozen bears, hurled her burden on a smoldering pile of stinking garbage, and retreated to watch.
>
> The largest of the bears, a sow weighing perhaps 400 pounds, waddled over, stood on the bag, splitting it open, and began nuzzling among the coffee grounds, tin cans, chicken bones and watermelon rinds.
>
> "Get its picture, Phil," said another woman. "Here, get me in it, too." She stood within 25 feet of the bear so her husband could get her and the bear in the same shot.[§]

Fifteen years after my family's 1968 visit to the dump, I approached the problem from the perspective of public policy. Now Governor James Blanchard's environmental policy advisor, I was influenced by front-page environmental news about the spreading contamination of groundwater. One of the most notorious culprits was the garbage landfill. Across the state, landfills were failing, discharging potentially dangerous chemicals into groundwater that supplied drinking water to thousands of citizens. Communities were up in arms about the siting of new dumps in their back yards. They wanted an end to landfills (not possible) and an increased emphasis on reducing, recycling and incinerating waste (possible).[¶]

We asked the Department of Natural Resources, responsible for landfill siting and enforcement, to provide a strategy for the governor to endorse. After some back-and-forth with the state's Department of Natural Resources (DNR), which wanted forty new unpopular waste incinerators, we settled on one. This plan

---

‡ "Garbage Dump Shutdown May Displace Bears," *Herald-Palladium* (St. Joseph, MI), June 24, 1982.

§ Thomas BeVier, "Up Town's Trash Brings the Bears—and Tourists," *Detroit Free Press*, August 10, 1986.

¶ I dealt with so many landfill and garbage issues as a governor's aide that my nickname became "Dave Dumpsite."

would concentrate on garbage reduction and recycling. While much of it was forward-looking, one of its pillars was the end to antiquated trash disposal methods.

The governor backed a proposal to fund the proper care and immediate closure of the dozens of remaining open dumps in the state. Hardly more than trash piles, with no underlying liners to prevent leakage, they were ticking time bombs. They not only threatened to spread contamination but also eroded public confidence. They had to go, and they would only go if the state paid for it. Most of the rural townships where open dumps flourished were too poor to foot the bill. In quick order, the legislature approved the money and sophisticated cleanup and monitoring requirements that went with it.

But the people of the Upper Peninsula are fiercely independent and often contrarian. In the case of the Copper Harbor dump, local officials continued to resist closure. Closing the dump would be like closing down the local state park or the most popular restaurant in town—a blow to tourism. Only seven years after the governor proposed using state funds to close open dumps did the Copper Harbor waste pile finally go out of business.

Closure of the dump does not equal closure to the issues it raised. What becomes of an animal's wild nature when it is conditioned by human beings to feast from our waste scraps? Is it still wild, or is it a tourism prop, like a circus animal? What does "wild" even mean when it comes to bears living practically side-by-side with humans? I have thought about all these things. I have few answers.

The Moose Drop

Within a few decades of Michigan's admittance into the union, gluttonous human appetites for its resources outran the supply and drove state officials to a new kind of management—the human propagation of said resources by government itself. In the 1870s, the Michigan Legislature created the Board of Fish Commissioners with the mandate to support fish stocks by building hatcheries and planting fish in the state's streams. Although initially only modestly successful, the program continued into the twentieth and twenty-first centuries. Hatcheries remain an indispensable tool in the sportfishing strategies of many states, including Michigan.

A rapidly increasing population and weak enforcement of the fish and game laws, nonetheless, depleted Michigan's bounty as the decades passed. State officials and sportsmen had another idea—the introduction of non-native species to create fishing opportunities. Brown trout came to the state's waters in 1883, imported by the U.S. Fish Commission. Native to Europe and parts of Asia, brown trout are now an accepted part of the state's fishery. The Michigan DNR says, "Brown trout are more tolerant of warmer water temperatures than other trout species, and as a result, browns have become the principal target of anglers in many rivers across the state, ranging from Michigan's best-known trophy waters to small, marginal trout streams in southern Michigan."[*]

Native only to Montana and Michigan of the contiguous forty-eight states, the exquisite cold water–dependent grayling was rapidly extirpated in the Great Lakes state. Each spring, lumberjacks pushed logs into the state's rivers after a winter of tree-cutting, smothering grayling breeding habitat with sand and, by exposing cold water rivers to direct sunlight, undermined the fish's survival. Grayling diminished rapidly from the 1880s on, and the last known to be caught in Michigan swam in the Otter River near Houghton in the 1930s. The state continues to attempt to reintroduce grayling, but so far, the experiments have failed.

A far more successful—and some said reckless—fishery experiment was the introduction of non-native salmon into Michigan's waters in the 1960s. Conceived as a strategy to eradicate undesirable, non-native alewives that the salmon consumed, the effort was also intended to create a lucrative sport fishery in Great Lakes waters that had grown sterile as a result of sea lamprey predation and lack of fishery agency interest. Described as "something spectacular" in the autobiography of Michigan's salmon strategy author, Howard Tanner, the program was a startling success, creating fishing madness—a crush of excited anglers competing to haul in the large anadromous fish as they massed to swim upriver from 1966 on. The fact that Michigan did not formally consult other Great Lakes states or Ontario before planting the salmon, and did not analyze all impacts, nettled some out-of-state fishery managers. But the success of the salmon introduction quieted their public objections.

Like other states, Michigan also attempted to restore native wildlife. Eradicated in the 1870s, elk made a comeback when the state imported seven animals from the West into north-central Lower Michigan in 1918. They thrived, growing to a population of around 1,500 in the early 1960s, before habitat loss and poaching reduced that to two hundred in the mid-1970s.

Oil exploration in the Pigeon River Country State Forest, key elk habitat, put the animals at the center of a court fight over protection of the area dubbed "The Big Wild." After compromises allowing regulated development while preserving habitat, the elk herd grew to over eight hundred by 1984. The population was deemed sufficient—and annoying enough to farmers whose crops elk plundered—that the Michigan DNR administered the first modern elk hunting season the same year.

---

[*] Michigan Department of Natural Resources, "Brown Trout," https://www.michigan.gov/dnr/0,4570,7-350-79135_79218_79614_82523--,00.html.

These successes emboldened natural resource managers. In the 1980s, I was witness to two more experiments. Each in its own way illustrated the need for human humility in the face of the wild.

The most dramatic and well-publicized wildlife reintroduction of the 1980s was the importation of Canadian moose to the Upper Peninsula (UP). Once native to both peninsulas of Michigan, the moose herd was extirpated from the Lower Peninsula before 1900 and nearly wiped out from the Upper two decades later. Everything from habitat (swamp and forest) destruction to brain worm disease spread by the expanding deer population was culpable.[†] A Michigan Department of Conservation UP moose reintroduction experiment in the 1930s failed.

The state's wildlife managers decided it was time again to try in the 1980s. The UP's deer population had substantially shrunk, reducing the risk of brain worm. This time, the Michigan Department of Natural Resources (DNR) turned to Canadian friends for a supply of moose.[‡] The two agencies collaborated on moose roundups in Algonquin Provincial Park in the winters of 1985 and 1987. The operation ran like clockwork. Staff darted moose with sedatives, slung them in nets under helicopters, and airlifted them to a staging area where biologists checked them out, fitted them with transmitter collars, injected them with drugs that reversed the sedatives, and packed them into crates. Trucks then transported the captured moose overnight approximately six hundred miles to prime identified moose habitat west of Marquette.

The 1985 moose lift—or "moose drop," as Governor Blanchard's UP representative Tom Baldini dubbed it—was a hit with the public. Members of sporting groups that had helped subsidize the operation turned out for the release of twenty-nine moose, but so did the public at large. Several thousand spectators attended the liberation of the gawky-looking moose.

Operation Moose Lift II took place in early February 1987. The first batch of moose had not included enough bulls to support the desired level of propagation. Moose Lift II was conceived of as a necessary element of a strategy to build a herd of one thousand UP moose by the year 2000.

This time, a special guest would observe the moose release. In Marquette for an event commemorating the beginning of his second term, Governor Blanchard

---

† Brain worm is the common name for a parasitic nematode, hosted by deer, that can burrow into the spinal cord or brain of a moose, often leading to abnormal behavior, paralysis, and death.

‡ It wasn't a one-way deal. The DNR provided 150 of Michigan's wild turkeys to the Ontario agency in exchange, restoring the animal to the province for the first time in eighty years.

agreed to attend and participate by opening the door on a crate to release the first moose.

Again, the crowd was large. Buttressing it this time were invitees to a second-term inaugural party in Marquette that night. Many wore semi-formal dress, including long coats, because the party would take place only a few hours later. Most stood beside the truck in which the moose were crated, keeping a respectful distance. I stood with others atop a small hill looking down on the back of the truck. The organizers had constructed a lane from the spot the moose would be released up the hill and into the woods.

The formal moose release began. With the help of a DNR staffer, the governor slid back the door of the crate and a dazed-looking bull moose stumbled down a ramp onto the snow-packed ground. He looked up the hill at the route intended for him, seemed to think about it, then wheeled and turned toward the well-dressed crowd standing in what they had thought was a safe zone. With startled cries, dozens of people scattered out of the moose's chosen path, their coat tails flapping comically, successfully escaping his at least seven-hundred-pound bulk. Once he wandered away, the relieved revelers let out their breath in collective laughter and exclamations.

The hope of the moose project has been partially fulfilled. A western UP moose herd exists where none had in a half-century, but the target of one thousand animals has not been met as of 2021. In 2019, the DNR estimated the herd at approximately five hundred moose. Brain worm initially took down more moose than expected. A warming climate may also be suppressing moose reproduction. Still, the herd is slowly growing.

Early 1987 could go down in Michigan history as the season of wildlife reintroduction. Only six weeks after the moose drop, the DNR invited the governor to another ceremony—the release of four dozen Szechuan pheasants in southern Michigan.

Unlike moose, pheasants are not native to Michigan. Sportsmen imported pheasants to the state in the 1890s. The first pheasant hunting season in Michigan occurred in 1925. By the 1950s, hunters were harvesting a million pheasants in Michigan every year. But the pheasant population plummeted, and by the mid-1980s hunters bagged fewer than 100,000 annually.

Like other hunting seasons, the fall pheasant take fostered family traditions that were fondly remembered years later. *Lansing State Journal* columnist John

Schneider called the first day of pheasant season in his childhood—October 20—"the high holy day for the hunters in my family."§

"There was only one thing to do on Oct. 20: Pile into a car, or two cars—their trunks filled with shotguns, shells, boots, brush-busting khaki-colored jackets, brown-bag lunches—and drive from Detroit to the cornfields of Webberville and Dansville," Schneider wrote. They were good hunting, he said, flushing from farm fields "in a heart-stopping explosion of fluttering wings." But the loss of pheasant habitat to development, and farm practices that eliminated pheasant cover by turning almost every square foot of plantable soil into cropland, contributed to the wipeout of the birds.

With that hunting heritage and the fees paid by hunters for licenses as incentives, the DNR spent much of the 1980s weighing different measures to restore pheasants. By 1987, the agency settled on the Chinese pheasant as an answer. March 16 was set as the date for the ceremonial release of the brood stock, born of eggs imported from China, and the Gregory State Game Area, forty miles southeast of Lansing, as the location.

It was a brisk late winter morning. In addition to the governor, the Chinese consul general from Chicago, the former U.S. Ambassador to China, several state legislators, and a gaggle of outdoor writers showed up.

All went well with the first few pheasants. The governor and the consul general successfully opened gates on small boxes in which the pheasants had been kept and the birds flapped themselves high into the sky and were gone. But a few pheasants in, one burst from his cage into the air and splattered a state senator and a DNR communications specialist with waste. The crowd erupted in laughter as the legislator wiped himself clean with a rag handed to him by a DNR employee.

It would be tempting to say the pheasant got the last laugh. Instead, Michigan's habitat and agricultural practices did. The Szechuan pheasants briefly flourished, but by the 1990s, they were gone. In 2015, hunters bagged slightly more than 22,000 pheasants. The bird's restoration has so far proven beyond the capacity of wildlife biologists.

The UP moose herd has survived thanks to the implicit permission of humankind. Instead of managing for a maximum deer population on the vast UP

---

§   John Schneider, "Dreams of the Glory Days of Pheasant Hunting Endure," *Lansing State Journal*, October 20, 2016, https://www.lansingstatejournal.com/.

public land estate to satisfy hunters, the DNR gave up the effort, opening a gap for moose. The Lower Peninsula pheasant, by contrast, has to survive in large measure on private lands. And humankind is generally not willing today to alter agriculture practices for the benefit of sportsmen.

Manipulating wildlife works in some instances, but nature and especially the ways of humanity, including the gobbling up of prime habitat, prevail in the end.

Dee Dee

Dee Dee was the first, and I remember the least about her. She was a gift. My parents gave me Dee Dee for my seventh or eighth birthday. Her name derived from my initials.

We thought she was fully domesticated, but one day a paperboy came to the front door to collect that week's payment. My grandfather, a babysitter that day, opened the door to deal with him. Dee Dee slipped by them both and romped out of sight. The lure of freedom was irresistible. Although I couldn't see her expression that day, I have known since dogs who made their break for daylight, and they seemed triumphant, enabled to express a concealed longing, no matter how well their humans treated them.

Ultimately, what was then known as the dogcatcher captured her. We retrieved her within twenty-four hours.

Responsibility came with the gift of a living being, and I wasn't up to it. She needed to be bathed, fed, and walked. Lazy at heart, I did little of it, so my mother gained a fourth child, one too many.

We adopted Dee Dee out—to a breeder. Last I heard of her, the breeder had dubbed her Lady Dempsey, and I believe she was producing healthy pups for others. I wonder whether she ever thought of us.

Wilderness

n my earliest days as an environmental advocate in the 1980s, my highest ambition was to protect what the Sierra Club and I called Michigan wilderness. I was so new to the field that I knew little of the etiology of the word "wilderness," let alone the emotionally charged Michigan politics associated with it.*

I did know that the first four letters of the word symbolized something to me and many others—the idea of a place untamed by humans, left alone to natural processes. In a world increasingly convulsed by people, I saw a virtue in setting aside land where structures, even motors were banned, where the pulse of one's body could match the pulse of nature. I assumed anyone with the environment at heart agreed.

I had done enough reading to know about the federal Wilderness Act of 1964, and the many laws establishing national forest wilderness in specific states since then. I didn't see why Michigan's vast national forests shouldn't have more wilderness areas.

---

* A substantial part of this chapter was inspired by William Cronon's essay, "The Trouble with Wilderness," in *Uncommon Ground: Rethinking the Human Place in Nature*, New York: W. W. Norton, 1996.

Not far into my career, just appointed to serve as the governor's environmental policy advisor, I got an education on the complexities of wilderness. It began when I received a call from the editor of the *North Woods Call*, Glen Sheppard. I had heard of him. He was Michigan's Old Man of the North Country. A Korean war veteran who enlisted when underage to be part of the fight, he was a passionate hunter, angler, and conservationist—a word that I hadn't thought about much.

Glen—affectionately known as Shep—was notorious for picking fights with bureaucrats and inventing quotes to round out his stories appropriately. But he was also something of a Michigan conservation conscience. From his bunker near Charlevoix, he issued cannonades of often angry prose attacking the sell-outs in the capitol. Shep described the *Call* as an "admittedly biased newspaper dedicated to the proposition that there is only one side in any issue involving resources—'NATURE'S.'"

On that first call, Shep did not waste any time (it turned out he never did) on the formalities. He invited me to his place for an interview and conversation about the state of Michigan's environment. I accepted.

I was nervous as I drove north three and a half hours from Lansing on a cool Friday night in September. He was a sportsman; I was at most a day hiker. I hadn't held a gun since firing a .22 at summer camp rifle range class between eighth and ninth grade, and I had no desire to hold one again. Shep frequently wrote of duck hunting, aided by his beloved bird dogs. I did feel confident of one skill. I was sure I would outdrink him, tapping from the fifth of Jack Daniels I had brought for us to share.

When I knocked on his door, I wasn't sure what I would see, but whatever it was, Shep wasn't it. His scalp shaved clean where there was hair, but otherwise mostly bald, he peered suspiciously at me through scuffed lenses. The test had begun.

He welcomed me coolly, guiding me to the living room, where his wife Mary Lou sat. After exchanging greetings with her, I followed Shep into a messy little box of a room anchored by a desk almost covered by leaning stacks of paper. Paper littered the floor. He took his desk chair and waved me to an upholstered chair battered by years of abuse. Stuffing poked from the back and seat cushion.

Shep asked me a single question—had I read the most recent *Call*?—before a half-hour lecture on conservation. The purpose of natural resources agencies, he said, was to assure resources weren't wasted—either by overuse or by disuse. And the agencies invariably screwed up. In the grip of lobbyists for the oil, timber, and mineral industries, the state Department of Natural Resources was often a whore whom only the citizenry could bridle. There was another threat, he said, "People like you." He then smiled and said, "Not you personally, just all your tree-hugging friends."

It's difficult to believe I was so uninformed about the history of the conservation and environmental movements to be surprised by his comment. To anyone who has worked in the field, it is a critical fact of life. It's a cultural divide. While the two camps occasionally cooperate where they have common interests—for example, protecting clean water for its own sake but also to assure aquatic habitat for healthy fish and wildlife populations to be "harvested"—they work side by side but rarely together. On most issues they have differing levels of interest, and, on a few, they clash. I was about to learn about one of those.

After a shot of Jack or two, I felt comfortable enough to turn the conversation to something I cared deeply about, and was confident he would too. I hoped to persuade Governor Blanchard to support a Michigan wilderness bill in Congress.

Snorting, Shep said, "Wilderness? There's none left. What are you talking about, wilderness?"

I bristled. "There's 90,000 acres of it in the bill."

"That's a sorry excuse for wilderness. Almost all of it was logged, and all of it is too small to be wilderness. How can a wilderness be a place where you can hear the traffic or see twenty or thirty hikers?"

"I doubt you can hear traffic," I retorted. "And as long as people don't drive through the woods in their pickups, and they leave nothing behind, that doesn't make it non-wilderness."

Shaking his head, he snapped at me—not unkindly, but like a teacher addressing a student who's a little slow. "That's pretty clear. Wilderness has to be big. It's tens or hundreds of thousands of acres where you can visit and get lost if you want to. Not these little manicured gardens you greenies want to save. But the big deal that you better be careful about is that wilderness is like waving a red flag in front of a bull. There ain't a single true conservation group in Michigan that'll support your boss on this."

I was annoyed. "What's wrong with them that they can't support such a common-sense thing?"

He sucked down another shot. "Because it's misuse, it's non-use. Wilderness the way you and your Sierra Club buddies look at it is sentimental. It's a bedtime story that puts you to sleep with a smile on your face. You people need to wake up. Resources are for using, not for locking up. Wilderness is an elitist idea—if you can even call it that. It's the cry of a baby."

If I had any skill at politics, it was knowing when to move on. I shifted the conversation to other subjects on which we were less likely to have sharp disagreement, and after a while, the liquor soaked up our aggression. We each retired before eleven.

I remember only one thing about the following day. Shep drove me in his pickup to a road end at Lake Michigan and told me to walk south. He would meet me where the trail ended, at another road end. A little puzzled, I agreed. Who could object to a Lake Michigan shoreline walk?

Like the topic of wilderness, the walk turned out to be a little more complicated than I expected. Water levels were high and, in some cases, there was little or no dry beach to traverse. I climbed inland, but there was no path. Drizzle dampened my hair and face. Branches of shrubs and low-hanging trees scraped at my cheeks. The going was slow, and generally unpleasant. But I had no choice.

More than three hours later, I came out at the road end to see Shep sitting in the cab of his pickup, reading something. He looked up and spotted me. As I climbed into my seat, he said with amusement, "A little surprised?"

"Damn you," I muttered. "You tricked me."

He shifted the truck into reverse and backed us around and then headed out. The engine groaned. "It was a test. You're a city boy. I wanted to see if you could take a little tough going."

I told him to buzz off, although in different language, and he laughed. The rest of the visit was uneventful.

When the *Call* arrived a week later, I was surprised to see a photo he'd taken on the front page. It looked as staged as it was. I was crouched beside a stream, running my hand through it the way you test a bath before stepping in. I looked about as much a fisherman or hunter as a politician in a three-piece suit. But what could he do with the material I gave him? At least his article was kind. Although observing that I did not participate in what he called the manly "blood sports," he also reported that I seemed to have the right instincts and values. (He made it clear that it was unlikely that I or the governor I served would ever rival the greatness of Blanchard's predecessor, William Milliken.) You could call it cautious optimism.

That doesn't mean he changed his mind on wilderness. He clung to his position and wrote skeptical columns and editorials on the subject for the next several years.

And back downstate in the capital, I soon learned how right he was about how charged the word "wilderness" was and is. Not just to the timber industry, which regarded the concept of wilderness as a crime against capitalism, but also to the conservationists. First among those in Lansing was the Michigan United

Conservation Clubs (MUCC). Headed by the unforgettable, coarse, but politically savvy Tom Washington, MUCC was firmly against federal legislation protecting Michigan wilderness. On one of my visits to his office habitat, foul with cigarette smoke and decorated with such office trophies as an ashtray atop a deer hoof and some kind of stuffed primate with a roll of toilet paper balanced in its two index fingers, he let me know I was creating trouble for my boss if I put him on record favoring wilderness.

"We're not in favor of locking up public lands," he growled. When I tried to interject, he waved at me to close my mouth and added, "Only elitists want to keep ORVs (off-road vehicles) off the public's land." I pointed out that the 90,000 acres was only about four percent of Michigan's federal forest lands and asked whether giving up motorized recreation on such a small estate was really a big sacrifice.

"Any limitation like that is an attack on freedom," Washington replied.

His position joined him with an unlikely ally, State Senator Joe Mack of Ironwood, Michigan, at the far west end of the Upper Peninsula. Notorious for opposing every environmental initiative since the dawn of time, Mack fiercely detested wilderness as "a creeping cancer." He once said, in support of timber harvesting as a way of cleaning up forests, "trees don't even have the decency to bury their dead." A wilderness meant a lot of dead bodies that would rot and fester.

Mack would have been easy to dismiss politically except that he was a Democrat like the governor. Governors need the votes of senators from their party to enact their programs, especially when only two votes divide the party caucuses. Despite this, and to his great credit, Blanchard announced his support for federal legislation designating national forest wilderness areas in Michigan. Inserted as a line in a speech to the Sierra Club on a Saturday night, it attracted the notice of a *Detroit Free Press* columnist named Hugh McDiarmid, who authored a whole column about it. Mack's outraged reaction was predictable and venomous. He didn't tell McDiarmid this, but he suspected the tree-hugger on the governor's staff was to blame. (It is fine when an aide takes the rap on something like this; a Mack type can persuade himself that it was the assistant, not the boss who offended him.)

The governor's support enabled the sponsor of the federal wilderness legislation, the principled, remarkably civil, and respected Congressman Dale Kildee of Flint, to schedule a hearing in the U.S. Capitol. I was dispatched to testify. I have two memories of the trip—first, as a provincial, being astonished to find a wall phone at sitting height beside the toilet in my hotel room and second, pleasing Congressman Kildee with the governor's unequivocal support for his bill.

The legislative journey wasn't quite done yet. The timber interests and MUCC's Washington pitched a fit, slowing the bill down in the 1985–1986 session of Congress. But early in 1987, the bill finally sailed through, and President Ronald Reagan signed it. His autograph on the bill wasn't a given—Reagan was not exactly environmentally conscious—but the legislation was probably too minor a matter to concern his aides. That was fortunate, because Washington, also a prime figure in the National Rifle Association, sent a telegram to Reagan's people urging him to veto the bill.

Mission accomplished, right? As the years have passed, that has become less and less clear, for several reasons.

It's appropriate to stop and see what the word "wilderness" means. In the 1964 Wilderness Act, which provided the framework for legislation like Michigan's, Congress defined wilderness thusly: "A wilderness, in contrast with those areas where man and his own works dominate the landscape, is hereby recognized as an area where the Earth and its community of life are untrammeled by man, where man himself is a visitor who does not remain." That's a much more generous characterization than one that prevailed earlier in European settlement of North America. In those days the adjective "howling" was often coupled to "wilderness," meaning "a wild, desolate place inhabited only by wild beasts." Wilderness was a place beyond the protection and comfort of the community, dark, even evil. Three hundred years later, its distance in miles and character from the human community would become a virtue.

But "howling wilderness" excluded part of that human community, just as the "discovery" of America by Columbus overlooked the millions of human beings who had peopled the continent. As the notion of wilderness evolved from frightful to Romantic, one characteristic did not change, the perception that it was an "untamed" land where "man himself is a visitor." But, in fact, men and women often did reside on, or make use of these lands for many generations before the Europeans arrived. Thus, the Michigan wilderness bill could be thought of as institutionalizing a land history that ignores those who dwelt here for millennia. At the very least, it conveys historical amnesia.

Most of the wilderness acreage that Congressman Kildee's bill protected was not "virgin" forest. The timber industry had logged the overwhelming majority of it. The second-growth or third-growth that now crowned it was an artifact of human and natural reforestation.

Then there's the problem of relentless human activity outside the boundaries of wilderness. No example better than climate change exists. When I thrilled at the idea of setting aside forest reserves, I was forgetting that the trees, the undergrowth, the creatures that inhabit them will not be static. As the Michigan climate warms and moistens, plants and trees native to ecosystems to the south will intrude on wilderness boundaries. In one hundred years, legally designated wilderness like the McCormack Tract in the western Upper Peninsula won't look or be anything like it is today.

What about the politics? Enacting a law designating wilderness areas does not secure them for all time. If the need for timber becomes a crisis, or runaway population growth demands more human living space in Michigan, a future Congress can amend or repeal the law. The bromide that there are no permanent victories in conservation is doubly true when the short-term victory is protection of a resource that somebody wants.

One of the objections that Shep expressed to me in our first meeting was the size of the ten protected areas. One, Nordhouse Dunes, is only 3,450 acres; the largest, Sylvania, is 18,300. In Shep's view, these were practically pocket parks. If you are going to protect wilderness, he said, it should be big and its heart difficult to access. Nordhouse Dunes is notable chiefly for protecting an undeveloped chunk of Lake Michigan shoreline. You can park in an asphalt lot, walk a few hundred yards in the sand, and cross the wilderness boundary. The smallest area protected by the law is the bulk of Round Island, which marks the busy junction of shipping lanes in the Straits of Mackinac. It is easily within sight of the tourist hub of Mackinac Island, visited by more than a million vacationers each year. A prominent and historically significant lighthouse rises from Round Island's western flank, and is technically not part of the wilderness. That it is an island means relatively few will visit it. But can a wilderness be so visually accessible, and its boundary marked by a building?

There's another side to the debate, of course. A persistent band of articulate advocates, led by Michigan's Sierra Club, including my friends Jane Elder and Anne Woiwode, crusaded for Michigan wilderness protection for over a decade. A small group of people made an outsized impact. They overcame resistance from the powerful timber lobby and from the conservationists. I cannot accept that they sacrificed for nothing.

What they preserved may not fit a standard definition of wilderness, or that of Glen Sheppard and Tom Washington, but it represents one of the finest of America's aspirations—to preserve the past so that we can understand the future. Advocating in the 1940s for the protection of a wilderness on state land, Porcupine Mountains, Michigan Governor Harry Kelly called it a "timber museum." Perhaps Michigan wilderness can be thought of in this way: a museum without walls, an aspect of the state that is worth preserving for its historical value, as much as or more than the Round Island Lighthouse, and enabling us to measure its change over time. That should be a common denominator. Some will see in it a refuge for peace and contemplation, others a playground shared with few, some a hiking or paddling challenge, and still others an anachronism founded on false assumptions—but we should all agree that it is a sample of state history that is also ever evolving.

Whether you think of it as wilderness or not, it keeps alive a conversation about a forest sustained for thousands of years, then consumed in little more than a generation by a growing (or greedy) society, then restored mostly by letting it alone. Protecting it was a worthy achievement.

The Bird of Peace

There's great wisdom in shunning the temptation to give personal advice to friends, family, and acquaintances. Offering advice requires arrogance, ignorance, or both. And it often results in misfortune for those who accept it. I've learned that from the experience of misguiding those I thought I was helping. Thus, it is a mild irony that the word "advisor" has been part of my job title for the majority of the last forty years.

I've been a policy advisor for the governor of Michigan, the Michigan Environmental Council, Clean Water Action, the International Joint Commission, and FLOW (For Love of Water). In that context, the title suggests giving an individual or an organization the best possible guidance on how to protect the environment through public policy initiatives. More pragmatically, while working for a politician, the job is to provide advice on how to maximize environmental achievements at minimum political cost. Ideally, advisors are thinkers, researchers, or networkers, collecting the best ideas, synthesizing them, testing them against political realities, and presenting them to decision-makers for endorsement. Significantly, advisors are not managers; they have little, if any, responsibility for implementing advice if it is embraced. One could say it's the best of both worlds, but it can also be the worst.

Early in my career, I thought of the job as strategy preparation. It wasn't a matter of the governor embracing one piece of legislation or policy. He could support a sweep of measures to deal with a threat like groundwater contamination or urban sprawl. These strategies could run scores of pages long and include unobjectionable, if unimpressive, proposals like improved groundwater data collection. Data are always underfunded in government budgets. What legislator or governor would be re-elected by running on the achievement of better data collection? Other proposals could be Jupiter-sized, like writing a new law protecting groundwater and preventing its contamination. Strategies had the advantage of guaranteeing at least a few minor accomplishments to obscure defeat on the major ideas.

The strategies conveyed, and were meant to convey, seriousness. What organization would turn out such a document if it wasn't committed to constructive policymaking? Merely presenting a stack of the reports at a news conference could impress the journalists and, perhaps, their readers and viewers.

That is the result in good times. But there are inevitably bad times, and I've been responsible for a few.

Beginning in the 1980s, Michigan's sportsman's lobby campaigned for the reclassification of mourning doves as a game animal and the opening of a regulated season in Michigan. They observed that neighboring Indiana (and dozens of other states) sanctioned a mourning dove season and that some Michigan hunters traveled there to hunt the birds, depriving the state of the commerce that could result from a season at home. Biologically, they argued, hunting the birds did nothing to undermine their reproduction rates. States with hunting seasons had abundant mourning dove populations. Hunting supporters said that although the meat on a mourning dove is limited, it is tasty. Finally, they argued, mourning doves were challenging to shoot. Their flight speed of up to sixty miles per hour and twisting and turning style made them tough targets.

No hunter myself, I was unenthusiastic about mourning dove hunting. But at the same time, the hunting lobby's logic and science seemed impeccable. And if you believe hunting has a place in our society, then mourning dove hunting also has such a place. I do respect hunting, done right—by others.

The forces opposed to mourning dove hunting were, if anything, more impassioned and determined. They expressed outrage. It would be simplistic to characterize the opposition as little old ladies in tennis shoes—but they were a loud part of it. Audubon Society members were particularly incensed.

The two lobbies inhabited different worlds. While Eric Sharp, the *Detroit Free Press* outdoor writer, was posting mourning dove recipes (best barbecued as an appetizer, or three to five birds, a full meal for an adult, served hot on triangles of buttered rye toast), Ronald and Leodora Bird (their real names) were writing a letter to the editor of the *Free Press* scoffing at the idea of "a 280-pound man or woman [taking] a 12-gauge shotgun and blowing away an 8-ounce bird for sport. Why stop there? Why not sponsor a bill to allow the hunting of anything that moves?"

That should have been a warning to me. But it wasn't, nor was a full page of anti–mourning dove hunting letters to the editor published in the newspaper as legislation to authorize a season lurched through the legislature. Sample:

> For those people mentioned in your article about dove hunting who claimed it would be a great family sport, I'd hate to see what else goes on in their households. What a great thing to teach your children, that it's fun and acceptable to kill things for no good reason. Yet everyone wonders why human violence is so out of control and getting worse.

Another warning sign was a public opinion poll conducted in the spring of 2004 finding that 50 percent of registered voters opposed hunting mourning doves, while only 31 percent approved. A candidate who scores 50 percent or better in a poll with a nineteen-point lead is generally on his or her way to a win.

But after almost twenty years of struggling with the issue, I decided that the biology should win. Emotions are one thing, but facts must rule, I concluded. Early in the first term of Governor Jennifer Granholm, as an outsider to her administration, but having endorsed her in the 2002 primary campaign, I publicly supported mourning dove hunting.

The arguments for a season were compelling, I told Granholm's aides. There wouldn't be too many other issues on which Granholm could attract the support of the typically Republican hunting and fishing lobby. If she stood up for the principle of science-based hunting policy, she might broaden her base a little. With a bill authorizing mourning dove hunting already introduced in and moving through the State House of Representatives, she would be under some pressure to declare herself.

The most prominent advisor supporting a season was Lieutenant Governor John Cherry, a hunter who was all for it. His opinion shaped the governor's.

The head of the Michigan United Conservation Clubs, Sam Washington, thought he saw a path to political daylight. His version of the bill would authorize an "experimental" three-year season in just seven of Michigan's eighty-three counties. Based on the results, the legislature could extend, expand, or end the experiment. I recommended she announce her support of the legislation. It was a compromise, after all. The hunters were giving something up.

Granholm's profession of support for the modified bill won some muted praise from sportsmen and their friends in the sporting press. It also stirred up howls of outrage from opponents of hunting mourning doves.

It turned out that while a candidate, Granholm had told the Michigan Humane Society that she did not favor a mourning dove season. Whether that amounted to a promise, or simply an expression of her views, soon became an object of emotional debate. To opponents of the dove season, there was no doubt it was a betrayal.

One letter writer professed to be "shocked and saddened" by the governor's turnabout. "When I voted for her, I did so believing she was a woman of her word." The writer concluded that one of the reasons the public was so skeptical of politicians was that they promised one thing and did another.

The governor signed the bill. It wasn't long before all hell broke loose. At an angry news conference less than two months after the bill took effect, organized anti-dove hunting advocates (Detroit and Michigan Audubon Societies, the Humane Society of the United States, and the American Society for the Prevention of Cruelty to Animals) promised to collect the 158,000 petition signatures needed to put the mourning dove hunting issue on the statewide ballot in November 2006. Under the state constitution, if they succeeded, the law would be put on hold, thereby cancelling the hunt in the fall of 2005 and 2006.

A leader of the coalition challenging the law spoke of fierce anger among many citizens about mourning dove hunting. Catering to them, the coalition showed reporters video of mourning doves dining demurely at backyard bird feeders, then "others being blasted by hunters in fields, with some birds flapping in their death throes."

Capitalizing on the visceral reaction to images like these—not offset much by the cool biological arguments in favor of hunting offered by sportsmen—the coalition easily secured enough signatures for a referendum. The secretary of state certified the signatures, eliminating the 2005 and 2006 experimental seasons.

In an online screed posted by an Audubon critic, I was cited as a traitor who had given away to killers the "bird of peace." It wouldn't have helped much if I had pointed out that the mourning dove is not the classic bird of peace—that distinction belongs to the dove generically. The Michigan Songbird Protection Coalition called the mourning dove "a peaceful bird which will swiftly fly from conflict on strong wings that make a whistling sound as they move through the air. The mourning dove plays a quiet, but vital role in the fragile and beautiful ecosystem that is the Michigan water wonderland." And now I and others wanted to allow people to shoot this symbol of nonviolence?

The imagery was far more compelling than the biology. In the November 2006 election, Michigan voters shot down the law by a whopping 69 to 31 percent margin. Fortunately, from my point of view, Granholm won re-election in the same statewide vote. Dove hunting was not a factor in her race.

The battle has continued since then—hunters and bird lovers are equally persistent—but there is still no mourning dove hunting in Michigan as of this writing.

What did I learn? The first lesson is clear—humility. No matter how many years you spend in policy and politics, you will always be surprised. Why, exactly, do Michiganders have such fierce antipathy to hunting mourning doves, while forty other states hunt the birds and seem to be functioning without domestic warfare? Each state, each community is a little different.

Another lesson is more of a reminder. It should be self-evident that, in a political contest between strong emotions and rational considerations, emotions will almost always win out. Contrast the mental image of a fluttering, cooing bird being shot out of the sky with the picture of an Excel spreadsheet documenting that populations of mourning doves in states with hunting seasons are stable or increasing. We typically make judgments on feelings or inclinations and, if necessary, find the reasons to support them.

The most important lesson of all, for me, is that we have come to love domesticated, even Romanticized, wildlife. The mourning dove is wild in a way not much different from my dog. The canine and I spend a lot more time together, but the dove isn't a stranger. She perches on my balcony rail, picks at seed fallen from the backyard feeder, barely moves until I am within a stride of her. She's adapted to humans, capitalizing on the habitat and food we inadvertently provide. She's omnipresent in the suburbs. For many people the mourning dove is a friend, a sign of peaceful constancy in a strife-torn world. And you can't successfully fight that.

Pudd'n

I met the seven-pound Pudd'n (obviously a name of Yorkshire provenance) as a college student on a weekend visit home during the fall semester of 1975. She instantly charmed me. Full of attitude all out of proportion to her size, she had a wire-trigger protective bark instinct and loved to play the game that I taught her—fetch. In less than two days at home, with several hours devoted to the task, we bonded over this. I sat on the kitchen floor and flung a plastic squeak toy in the form of a rolled-up newspaper down the hallway to the front door. She quickly got the idea, and proudly returned with the toy time after time. This made sense—the encyclopedia informed me that Yorkies were bred to catch mice and rats.

At least one trait suggested she was more than a lapdog, that she had a vestigial wild side. In those years, the Lansing newspaper was an afternoon edition. A paperboy dropped it off on weekdays between four and five, depositing it between the front door and the storm door. Within weeks of joining the household, Pudd'n discovered this ritual and invented a corresponding one. At mid-afternoon she perched on the lowest of the stairs descending from the second floor, her nose almost touching the crack between the front door and its frame. Her patience was Olympian. An hour, sometimes two, passed before the reward.

And what was that? The afternoon *Lansing State Journal*, of course. As soon as one of us opened the door she would growl menacingly and attack the newspaper. If we were not quick enough to intercede on behalf of the *State Journal*, she would sink her teeth into it and throttle it the way a Yorkie would presumably shake a mouse to death. This wasn't one shake—it was an angry, violent execution, with several pages of the paper often ending up in shreds. The job done, she would look up for approval, her tail going and her breath heaving. She interfered with our reading but how could we hold it against her? It was comical, endearing, and utterly natural.

Mortality

W hen I transitioned from executive director (and only staff person) of the nonprofit Michigan Environmental Council to an environmental policy advisor on the staff of Governor Blanchard in June 1983, I didn't know what I was getting into. I'm glad I had the opportunity, but it resulted in a rough schooling.

My model of a public servant was formed at home. In my childhood, my father moved from college professor to agency administrator. I admired his ideals. He considered himself to be making an important contribution to society, especially when he managed Michigan's gargantuan human services agency. There was another side to the idealist. Capitol observers described him as a savvy political operator who knew how to fight and win internal battles in the executive branch—for example, to get more money for his agency's budget—and duels with the legislature. High-minded principles and the bureaucratic equivalent of street fighting combined to keep him in government for over thirteen years.

At home, in dinner table conversations, I saw chiefly the idealism. Despite the occasional complaint about this or that human obstacle to his goals, my father typically spoke of his job in its human impact: working to support families with food, heating, and other assistance, and providing incentives for the indigent to return to self-sufficiency.

With his ideals came great pride in his reputation for integrity. He valued the regard of colleagues and journalists who thought him incorruptible. Once and only once during his service, headlines accused him of ethical violations for hiring someone with virtually no qualifications for political reasons. I had never seen him so hurt, so emotionally flattened before. This powerfully affected me. In the end, he was cleared, but the controversy left a wound.

My father literally worked (and smoked) himself to death at the age of fifty-seven. He thrived through the long days, deep nights, weekend work and weight of his decisions for most of his time in government, but these ultimately drained his physical reserves. He refused to slow down much after his lung cancer diagnosis, continuing to work even when a procedure that damaged his voice box silenced him for a time, determined to keep bravely at his post until it simply became impossible.

A vivid memory of his final weeks in the hospital was watching him dream. He slipped away from a conversation with me into a restless sleep. He began murmuring, his eyebrows lifting and falling, his hands jerking a little. I leaned over to make out what he was saying. I realized he was running a meeting.

His fate was terrible and drained me for a year or more until one day I became intensely angry for no reason at all. Well, that's not exactly true. My temper sizzled after I saw a man on the street who looked just like my father. For a few weeks after, I resented the living and the dead—including my father, for leaving us too soon. I had to ask: was it worth it to him and to us to give his life to the public? He was a martyr but also a robber, for he had gone away before we had a chance to know him as fellow adults, to resolve the inevitable childhood grievances, and to build a friendship.

My grieving, coincidentally, ended at about the same time I joined the governor's staff, fourteen months after my father's death. Without really being aware of it, I was ready to sacrifice myself, too. Martyrdom has a sort of Romantic appeal.

I'm glad I never forgot how I got the lucky break to work close to the center of the governmental solar system: by luck and default. Early in his first term, which began on New Year's Day 1983, my boss was pounded by journalists for having no positive environmental agenda, in contrast to his predecessor.

One reason he lacked an agenda was that he lacked a staff person devoted to environmental policy. Searching for one, his policy director turned to me because she knew of me from political campaigns. She knew I was green (as in lacking experience, not as an environmentalist), but that was not necessarily a bad thing in an office atmosphere characterized by the governor's desire to keep a rein on things, take few political chances, and, most of all, do nothing to increase the tax burden. In a struggling state economy where unemployment had reached 17 percent not long before, tax increases were as unpopular as they were necessary to keep the state's government from becoming bankrupt. The governor had narrowly squeezed an income tax increase through the legislature in his first months, but the payback was instantaneous. The opposing Republicans organized campaigns to recall from office the two swing Democratic votes in the state senate, and their success enabled them to take control of the senate and gain the power to stalemate much of the governor's remaining policy agenda.

What that meant for me was no proposals or promises to spend more money on combating air and water pollution and a multitude of other needs. In a sense, my mandate was doing as little as possible while maintaining constructive relationships with the key environmental and hunting and fishing constituencies.

What I wasn't expecting was the crisis of public confidence in government's ability to protect people from environmental toxins that was peaking at that moment in history. It would immediately shape my thinking—and feeling—about public service.

On my first full day on the governor's staff, having gotten directions to the coffee pot and the washroom, I was told about a dangerous environmental contamination problem in the Battle Creek area. Not long before, government agencies had confirmed the presence of toxic chemical solvents in the well water of the Verona neighborhood just outside the city. As was (and too often still is) typically the case, the wells of ordinary citizens served as pollution monitors. At first alarmed and later angry, they demanded the investigation that led to an environmental crisis.

Just before I joined the staff, thirty-five residents of the neighborhood had come to the capitol to demand to see the governor. They were turned away at the end of the workday. That weekend, the Battle Creek newspaper published a photograph of a sign on the roof of the protest's leader: "Gov. Blanchard—we came to you for help—we mistook you for someone who cares—if you don't come to us in person in 7 days we join recall effort."

The governor's chief of staff instructed me to get on it before seven days passed.

The neighborhood's wells lay between several suspected contamination sources—a landfill, a solvent facility, and a railroad maintenance garage—and the public water wells serving tens of thousands of customers in the community. In effect, the residents of the neighborhood served as the proverbial canary in the coal mine, becoming the early warning of a menace to the entire region. It was not lost on either the neighborhood or the government agencies that poison in the Battle Creek public water supply might mean a threat, including a public relations catastrophe, for the region's largest employer, Kellogg's.

The wheels of government, even in crises, turn slowly. As hydrogeological studies proceeded in an attempt to pinpoint the sources of the contaminated groundwater, and technicians mulled over how best to stop it from ruining the entire community's well field, the neighborhood's residents fumed. They wanted to know how long they'd been exposed to trichloroethylene, or TCE, what its health effects were, who was going to do something about it, and who was going to be punished.

The people of Michigan were even more sensitized than those of other states to chemical contamination. A decade before, an industrial accident introduced a toxic flame retardant into cattle feed, the first link in a chain that led to PBB exposure through the food chain for virtually every citizen in Michigan. The science on human health effects of PBB was weak. No one could be sure whether cancer, birth defects, or other dangers loomed. But one thing was clear: government had failed in its duty to protect the public.

With that in the background, the neighborhood residents already exposed to TCE were not settling for calm assurances from government employees that health risks were minimal. Nor should they have; the science was inconclusive but suggestive of potentially significant impacts. In 1977, the federal Food and Drug Administration had banned the use of TCE in food, cosmetic, and drug products while permitting its use as an industrial degreaser to continue. TCE had been used as an anesthetic for dental and surgical procedures and in veterinary medicine, an extraction solvent for natural fats and oils (such as palm, coconut, and soybean oils), and for spices, hops, and the decaffeination of coffee. What the government had ultimately determined was too risky to put in the mouths of Americans had entered these people through the tap.

In communities facing toxic chemical exposures, there are people with serious health problems, just as there are in every community across the country. But the chemically exposed communities often harbor what public health officials call "cancer clusters," or unusual concentrations of other effects. Given the state of knowledge then and now, it is almost impossible to draw a scientifically strong link between the exposure and the disease. To do so, one would have to know whether the affected people could have been exposed to the chemical and for how long, whether they were also exposed to other chemicals, what the incidence of the disease was in that family over the generations, the rate of such disease in a "control" community with the same demographics but no chemical exposure, and whether the scientific literature had anything conclusive to say.

This was the setting as I walked into my first public meeting with an outraged citizenry during my time in the governor's office. It was taking place in the community center, a windowless concrete box. Perhaps one hundred people filled uneven rows of metal folding chairs. The air inside the room sizzled with anger. I saw accusing, hostile expressions on the face of every neighborhood resident in that room. I said nothing at first, but resented being found guilty before a trial.

Something else was plain. This was a working-class neighborhood. These people mostly sweated for their paychecks, a condition from which my now thoroughly middle-class family was two generations removed. I wished I had driven through the neighborhood before showing up at this community center. I might have been better prepared.

It was my job to chair the meeting. I welcomed the audience, introduced the other three government presenters, and began to outline the evening's agenda when a man in the front row, wearing dark horn-rimmed glasses, jumped up and interrupted me.

"So you're gonna set the agenda? Typical government attitude. Treat us second-class. Not as good as yourselves."

I tried to conceal my annoyance. I was on his side. Why did he instantly try to make us enemies?

"Sorry," I said. "What would you like on the agenda?

"It's not just me, it's everyone in here," he said, turning and sweeping his arm in a 180-degree gesture. "It's our health, it's our property values, it should be *our* meeting." Many in the audience nodded or voiced their agreement.

When I am flustered, I make foolish judgments, and I was approaching one. This fellow was a bomb-thrower, not constructive, I decided. But I refrained from exploding. Having never faced an audience like this, I was floundering. I managed to croak out, "If it was your meeting, what would you do with it?"

His eyes fixed on me as if I were the source of his neighborhood's woes. "I'd ask you to stop giving excuses. Stop telling us everything's going to be fine, that the problem's all in our heads. And I'd tell you to get off your ass and do something to protect our health!" More nods from the audience.

I was close to blowing my top. I grasped at a straw. "Let's talk about that, but first, can you tell me who you are?"

This skinny man roared back at me, "John Niles, and I live here!"[*]

I cringed but tried to conceal it. "I respect that. I know this is a hard time for you and everyone here and in the neighborhood."

"Oh, I'm sure we appreciate your concern," he said. "You're just another apologist for the polluters and the bureaucrats."

I'd had it. "Now I resent that," I spluttered. "You don't know anything about me. This is the first time we've met, and you're judging me? I resent you or anyone questioning my integrity. What gives you the right?"

Now I felt my co-presenters shifting uncomfortably in their seats. I realized my blunder. So did Mr. Niles. He was enraged.

"What gives YOU the right to come in here and act all high and mighty?" he demanded. "You're not drinking and showering in poison. You're not getting sick because somebody didn't do their job or just didn't give a damn about other human beings. I've got leukemia, and I'm not the only one who's sick. We have kids with cancer, all kinds of sickness. It's our lives on the line."[†]

More nods, mutters, and murmurs. I broke out in a cold sweat. Suddenly providence intervened. In the back of the room rose a middle-aged woman with ink-black hair, and who, without being recognized, followed Niles with barely a pause.

"John, please give the man a chance."

Calming immediately, Niles turned to face her. "You're always the kind one. Damn it, Karen, you just sucked the wind out of my sails." He smiled.

"It's your sails that suck," Karen laughed. A few in the audience scowled but the rest chuckled. The tension was broken the way a fever breaks. "He's young," she said, looking my way. "Young people need to be educated, not judged, right? Give the man a chance." She sat down.

Niles remained standing, but the anger had drained from him. "All right, Karen," he said. "If he gives us a chance, we'll give him a chance." He turned to face me again. "We get to set the agenda, OK?"

"We're public servants, we're your servants," I smiled, and the tension eased further.

---

[*] This was not his name. I've changed it to protect his privacy.

[†] I later learned that Niles's tissue was tested by a private laboratory and found to have high levels of four toxic chemicals, including TCE.

"Now you're getting educated," Karen yelled from the back. I joined the laughter.

From there, the meeting proceeded generally peacefully. Niles built an agenda quickly with help from the neighborhood. They wanted their health questions answered. They wanted to know what progress the state had made in holding the polluters accountable. They wanted to know what we were going to do to get them clean water. With the help of the other presenters, I answered them the best I could. The audience wasn't always satisfied, but there were no outbursts. I made one commitment on top of promising to be open: I would figure out some way to get them clean water to drink and bathe in, at state expense, as soon as possible. I had no idea how I would do that or whether it was fiscally possible, but sheer humanity required me to try.

After nearly three hours, the meeting adjourned with my promise to communicate regularly with Niles and Karen as representatives of the neighborhood. That seemed to reassure the group. I was looking down and taking deep breaths as I collected the remaining papers of those I had brought to stuff in my briefcase when I sensed somebody waiting for me. I looked up to see Niles. Something in his air told me our trouble hadn't been resolved. He suggested we move over to the side of the room, and I agreed.

When we had enough distance for privacy he said, "You're lucky Karen was here or I'd have kicked your ass from here to eternity." There was anger in his eyes.

"You already did," I replied, trying to sound light.

"Look, just keep in mind one thing. You're not my friend, the government's not my friend, the corporations aren't my friend, you and they aren't the friends of anyone in this room. The proof's in the pudding. If you deliver on your promises, I'll keep my mouth pretty much closed. If you don't, you will see you've never had a worse enemy in your life." He was leaning into me, his face looming large, a finger jabbing at me. I was perspiring again.

"I hear you," I said, and I meant it.

"You better. You people are all against me, you're against my neighbors. You're full of talk. No BS, Dempsey, or else."

"Uh-huh."

He backed off a bit, the tension in his body dissipating. He breathed rapidly and shallowly for a few moments, looked me in the eye and stomped away.

Motivated as much by political fear as by humanity, government belatedly came through for the neighborhood. With the help of an administrator in the state Department of Natural Resources, I was able to find the funds enabling the governor to authorize bottled water and portable showers for the affected residences. The U.S. Environmental Protection Agency moved swiftly to drill intercept wells that stopped the groundwater pollution from reaching the municipal wells.

My co-presenters persuaded me to join them for a stop at a bar on the way back to Lansing, distant enough from the Verona neighborhood to run no risk of being noticed and questioned. As we sipped our beer, Mike, a public health agency section chief, who looked like Papa Hemingway thanks to his lush gray-white beard, began counseling me gently.

"You handled the meeting pretty well, congratulations," he said. "Good for a first time out on behalf of a governor."

Grateful for his words and the kindness in his manner, I said, "But what?"

"It probably isn't the best idea to fire back when you're talking to an angry mob. When one of 'em lobs a grenade at you, you can't throw it back. You've got to throw yourself on it and take the explosion. Except you'll live." The others nodded.

My face reddened. I wanted to defend myself, but I couldn't. "Well, it didn't go over well. That's for sure," I said.

Mike looked at me earnestly while sliding his glass full of beer between his hands. "That man, John, he's not angry just at you or the state, he's angry about dying young. He's coming to terms with his mortality under the worst possible circumstances."

Surprised, I mulled that over for a few moments. "I hadn't thought of that."

"I'm thirty years older than you and I hope I have another thirty. He's probably roughly my age. He wants another thirty. He's got cancer. Chances are the TCE has nothing to do with it. He's smoked since high school maybe. But he needs to find a reason, an enemy, outside himself."

I disagreed with his assessment of TCE. It was a known carcinogen, after all. How could he dismiss it? I was coming to realize that this was the public health community's conventional wisdom at the time.

But I was also coming to realize that I had a lot to learn about human nature, and that I was very, very young and inexperienced.

My father had died only fifteen months before. What had he felt as he descended into the acute phase of his cancer? At fifty-seven, he must have felt cheated and angry. And so did John.

I never acted that way in a public meeting again.

Landfill in the Sky

There was a time in the public policy world when a front-page story in the morning newspaper could stampede legislators and bureaucrats into action. I worked during the latter part of that period. I joined the scramble several times.

By 1986, the City of Detroit was nearing its tenth year of planning for and construction of a $470 million garbage incinerator, one of the biggest in the world. In 1984, it had received a Clean Air Act permit from the Department of Natural Resources (DNR). Now the DNR said it had made a mistake. DNR had inadvertently underestimated the cancer risk to those breathing its emissions. It requested that the city add sophisticated pollution control equipment.

The front-page headline in the morning *Detroit Free Press* of April 4, 1986, cried out, "DNR: Trash Plant Raises Cancer Risk." If anything, the content of the jump page, 15A, was more alarming. It displayed a map of Detroit with concentric rings, showing who would bear the brunt of the cancer risk per one million people: thirty-six adjacent to the incinerator site in Detroit, thirty in a nearby portion of Detroit and Hamtramck, and five in a stripe running through the suburbs from St. Clair Shores to River Rouge. Readers could compare the risk of breathing dioxins, heavy metals, and acid gases to their area of residence.

In an adjacent story on 15A, the situation grew murkier, like an opaque sky. A toxicologist for the state Department of Public Health had run the numbers and calculated a maximum additional cancer risk, closest to the incinerator, of seven in a million. Two state agencies, the Department of Natural Resources (DNR) and Public Health, were openly disagreeing—seemingly—on the health threat posed by the City of Detroit's massive trash incinerator.

The adjacent story also described the assumptions under which the agencies calculated the highest risk: it would accrue to a theoretical person living one and a half miles from the burner breathing the maximum amount of pollutants authorized by the state permit for seventy years, twenty-four hours a day. These were extraordinarily conservative assumptions under which DNR policy was to authorize a maximum additional risk of one in a million—but they were assumptions that I had personally supported until then.

So how had the two state toxicologists arrived at different estimates? The DNR toxicologist had extrapolated risk from laboratory rats to humans using body surface, while the public health toxicologist had extrapolated using body weight. The U.S. Environmental Protection Agency accepted the former, the federal Centers for Disease Control the latter method. Meanwhile, a toxicologist retained by the City of Detroit calculated the risk to be below one in a million.

To journalists and the public, the difference in assessments was stark. DNR was estimating more than five times additional cancers than was the Department of Public Health. But in the community of risk assessors, the gap was negligible. When the inexact science delivered results within the same order of magnitude, they were essentially saying the same thing.

The Detroit incinerator had once enjoyed the support of state government. At its inception, the state had supported its construction as a safe alternative to dumping trash in landfills. Now a branch of that government considered it a toxic menace, a landfill in the sky that the public would inhale.

According to the financially struggling city, an additional $17 million in capital costs for additional air pollution control equipment and $8 million in annual operating costs loomed because the DNR had changed its mind. City officials, who thought the DNR had given its final approval to the incinerator in 1984, were livid. Bella Marshall, Detroit's finance director, accused the DNR staff of, in effect, lying, and added that their falsehoods called "their morals and ethics into high question."

The governor, as the superintendent of the executive branch of state government, was expected by municipal officials to settle disputes among his agencies.

The particular municipality involved in this dispute was headed by Detroit Mayor Coleman Young, a Black Democrat who could turn out (or not) the city's vote in Blanchard's bid for re-election seven months later. I don't know whether the communication was direct between the two, and there was no direct communication from the governor to me about a course of action, but I absorbed the directive.

Like everyone else involved, I read the paper. A few weeks before the cancer risk map was displayed to the world, the governor had told the press, "You don't stop the whole project because you find something that might improve it later on." He added, "someone in the DNR tried to change the rules in the middle of the game." Later in the year, he would accuse the DNR of harboring "bungling bureaucrats."

Conversely, the chair of the state's Air Pollution Control Commission, a respected state public health administrator, phoned me the day of the *Free Press* article and said, "Dave, we *have* to require the equipment," referring to the scrubber and baghouse technology that would back up the already mandated electrostatic precipitator. Normally even-toned, his voice expressed agitation. He referred to the cancer risk map in the newspaper. "People won't tolerate this."

Further complicating the situation was the fact that a nearly all-white State of Michigan air pollution bureaucracy was trying to tell a city whose residents were approximately 75 percent Black to spend more money for what Detroit saw as an unnecessary investment to deal with a nonexistent risk. For me, still another twist was that my friends in the environmental community considered the issue a litmus test of the governor's environmental values, and expected him and me to stand up for the DNR.

That was never going to happen.

Instead, I conveyed via conversations, winks and nods—nothing in writing—that the governor wanted the state to stick to the original permit and spare the city millions of dollars. Easiest to convince this way were three state employees on the Air Pollution Control Commission, which would make the official decision on the air-quality permit. They understood the message I was sending without saying so explicitly. The governor was their boss, and he wanted the project to go ahead and the original permit to remain in force.

But those were only three votes on an eleven-person commission. And while members sympathetic to industry and municipalities filled several of the remaining seats, there were just enough members whose votes were unpredictable to leave the outcome dangling. I could not be even indirect with them; they might tell reporters the governor was leaning on them.

Such was the setup when the commission convened in Detroit on April 9, 1986. It was one of the most extraordinary public meetings I've attended. Four hundred people packed the auditorium. Police turned away another one hundred. Outside, picketers bore signs. One said, "Burn Politicians, Not Garbage," another "Trash the Incinerator."

But this was not yet a clear-cut environmental justice issue. A large number of Black Detroit residents, many turned out by Mayor Young's team, said they favored the incinerator and wanted the state to stop meddling in the city's business. Many opponents of the incinerator were white environmentalists from outside the city.

The hall was charged with anger. Jeers and catcalls responded to testimony on both sides. Tucked in the back of the auditorium, I came upon one of my environmental advocate friends who strongly opposed the incinerator. We locked eyes angrily and challenged each other. I was now in this emotionally all the way—supporting the incinerator. I had never expected it to come to that.

Testimony continued until 3 a.m. When it was done, a representative of Attorney General Frank Kelley said proponents of the extra pollution control equipment had made a weak case. Astonishingly, after seven and a half hours, he said the commission had no legal authority to revoke the original permit anyway. By a nine to one vote, the commission quickly ended the discussion and affirmed the 1984 permit.

Back in the office the next day, the governor's chief of staff warmly congratulated me on delivering what our boss wanted. I tried, but not too hard, to say I hadn't had much to do with it.

The back-patting didn't last long. A little more than twenty-four hours after the commission's vote, U.S. EPA staff in Chicago told journalists they had planned to attend the Detroit meeting, but a cancelled flight had kept them away. Had they attended, they would have argued in favor of the more protective air pollution control equipment. Now they said they wouldn't rule out legal action to force the city's hand.

The battle did eventually end up in the courts. The outcome was unclear for a while, but eventually the city was forced to install the sophisticated pollution control equipment.

Another outcome was immediately clear. The director of the DNR, Ronald Skoog, resigned. Many, including the governor, faulted Skoog for not controlling his staff. I was dispatched to his office in a state office building to send a message from the governor.[*]

---

[*] The governor had never wanted Skoog to direct the DNR. In the 1980s, an independent Natural Resources Commission hired and fired the DNR director. A majority of commissioners appointed by the previous governor served when, in 1983, the director's position was vacated. Over Blanchard's objections, the commission picked Skoog.

He closed the door to his lair and sat across from me at a conference table. Before I could say anything beyond a greeting, he pushed a book across the table to me and began earnestly explaining it. The title was *Hands-Off Management*. He was a believer that an organization's employees grew fastest if they were allowed to act and learn without too much interference from above. This summarized, to me, exactly why the governor thought him unfit. But Skoog's sincerity touched me.

He looked me in the eye and asked me if he had the governor's support. I shook my head. He was fifty-nine, I was twenty-nine. It was like firing my father.

Once the incinerator opened, it was undeniably an environmental justice issue. Residents of the surrounding neighborhood, who had never wanted the burner, paid the price for its chronic malfunctions and noncompliance with the law. When the incinerator finally shut down in 2019, thirty years after it opened, a newspaper columnist called it "despised." It had become the scourge of the community, its foul odors and noise sickening a mostly Black populace.

Between 2013 and 2018, the burner violated its air pollution permit 750 times. An EPA document said the neighborhood had become a hotspot for respiratory-related health impacts when compared to other Michigan communities. Its closure was a major step forward for public health. I had planted my feet on the wrong side of environmental history.

Finally, the political outcome would provide mixed results. Never close, Blanchard and Young co-existed in 1986. The city's voters turned out and the governor won a landslide re-election. But four years later, when Blanchard sought a third term, he had lost the mayor's support. This time Detroit voters didn't turn out, and in a narrow but shocking upset, Blanchard lost the 1990 election.

The only winner, for decades, was the Detroit incinerator.

The Fight over Flowers

The business of naming official state symbols is surprisingly complicated. What seems at first an opportunity to boast about the special features of a place—physical, natural, and cultural—often becomes a struggle between constituencies arguing that their emblem is better than the other guy's.

States take different approaches to the naming of symbols. In the two states where I've spent most of my life, one has been liberal in designating symbols, one a little choosier. Minnesota has twenty-two, including a state bird (the common loon), a state muffin (blueberry), and a state photograph (*Grace*). Legislators rejected a bid to make the official state amusement ride the Tilt-a-Whirl, which was invented in Faribault. A tongue-in-cheek proposal to make the mosquito the official state insect did not survive the legislative process.

Michigan's state symbols are slightly fewer (eighteen) and generally more conventional. There is a state bird (robin), state stone (Petoskey), and state reptile (the painted turtle). There is a state soil (Kalkaska series), a state tree (the Eastern White Pine), and a state song ("My Michigan").

But the story behind the official Michigan wildflower, which I witnessed at close range in the state capitol in the 1990s, is a story of surprising passions and a rivalry that generated ill will. It also has something to say about what is wild and what is not.

The history of the battle over the official state *wild*flower cannot overlook the fact that since 1897, Michigan has had an official state flower, the apple blossom. Of course, the proliferation and management of the apple blossom is today primarily a matter of cultivation, not wild growth. That left open the door for a wildflower contest between trillium and the dwarf lake iris.

I can see the value of trillium, with its lovely three white petals. Each spring, my hopes rise with its emergence on the floors of forests whose trees are not yet fully leafed out. Their typical appearance in May is a clear sign that the long gray months are over. It presages the joy of summer and is a reminder of the renewal of the Earth.

The dwarf lake iris (*iris lacustris*) has its own selling points. First, approximately 90 percent of its global population grows in Michigan, primarily along the northern shores of Lakes Huron and Michigan, a reason why it is listed as a threatened species under the federal Endangered Species Act.[*] Its habitat being so close to the two lakes has rendered it vulnerable to destruction as home development colonizes coastal areas. The trillium has no abundance problem. Thirty-eight species of trillium grow across North America.

Second, dwarf lake iris is a thrilling little plant. Its subtlety is expressed in its quiet beauty. Its diminutive deep blue flowers are about one to one and a half inches in width and one and a half to two and a half inches in height. They create picturesque carpets of color during springtime blooming just inland from the beaches of the two Great Lakes. Because it is small, delicate, and rare, the iris inspires protectiveness, which means its defenders can be fierce.

Enter Kathleen Thomson. A tall, loud, and persistent champion of the dwarf lake iris, she was an activist in the Michigan Botanical Club. Born in New Mexico, which inspired her to become a cactus hobbyist, and later a resident of Wisconsin, she moved with her husband to Michigan in 1966. She became what she termed "a plant conservationist."

Kathleen approached Ann Arbor State Senator Elizabeth Brater to sponsor legislation recognizing the dwarf lake iris as the latest state symbol. But the Michigan Wildflower Association had organized mail-in balloting through newspapers offering voters a choice of six flowers (including the round-lobed hepatica,

---

[*] Almost all of the remaining population grows along the shores of Lakes Michigan and Huron in Wisconsin and Ontario.

bloodroot, Michigan lily, and wild lupine) to get the honor. When the results were tallied, the trillium defeated the dwarf lake iris, 1,773 to 1,479, with the others trailing badly. The association considered holding a runoff election between the two, but decided against it.

That didn't faze Kathleen. She spoke to garden clubs and visited plant nurseries, circulating petitions. She charged ahead on the Brater bill, angering Lou Twardzik, president of the Wildflower Association. He called Kathleen's determination to move ahead with the dwarf lake iris "an outrageous power play by select environmental interests over the interests of the people of Michigan."[†]

In fact, it was a power play, but not outrageous, by Kathleen Thomson. No environmental interests got seriously involved in backing the legislation. As a lobbyist for the Michigan Environmental Council (MEC), I limited my role to offering a little advice when she asked for it, and turning in a card at a legislative committee meeting with MEC's support indicated. With what one reporter called "an evangelist's zeal," Kathleen did most of the phone calling and testifying and much of the publicity.

The fact that she was not a fixture in the capitol on any other issue worked in her favor. She didn't know when she was breaking legislative etiquette and probably wouldn't have cared if she had; she had an excuse for violating the norms preferred by politicians. In particular, she harangued some lawmakers more than they were accustomed to, prompting a fair amount of eye-rolling. Kathleen had a low opinion of legislators' characters but an unconditional love for the character of the flower that she fought to protect.

Despite grumbling from a handful of legislators in both the state senate and house about the issue wasting their time, the bill designating the dwarf lake iris as the official state wildflower cleared the legislature in December 1998. Now the question became: would Governor John Engler, who had expressed skepticism about the need for more state symbols, veto the bill? He did not. His press secretary said that when the bill was presented to Engler, he said, "Why are we doing this?" But he signed it anyway. After all, he had signed into law the painted turtle as the state reptile.

The happy end to Kathleen's effort finally settled the matter. Mostly. Twardzik of the Michigan Wildflower Association grumbled, "The dwarf lake iris is an isolated plant that grows in remote places of the state seen by a few. The trillium glorifies

---

† Marty Hair, "Lawmakers to Debate Merits of Dwarf Lake Iris," *Detroit Free Press*, October 4, 1997, p. 3.

the state everywhere for everybody." Meanwhile, Kathleen modestly shared the credit. "It's not a personal victory," she said. "Without the help of all these people, I couldn't have moved anything."

There has been no movement to repeal the designation. In her 2017 obituary, Kathleen's successful fight on behalf of the wildflower was noted as one of her life's great accomplishments.

What does it mean to celebrate flowers that are wild? To the extent the word "wild" has any meaning, like that which we typically ascribe to it, wildflowers own it. They typically exist independent of humankind in habitats they have preferred for centuries. They are here not because of humans, but in spite of them.

Yet that's the catch. Dwarf lake iris and many other threatened and endangered species exist, in a sense, because of human restraint, intentional or otherwise. Purchase of public lands that contain dwarf lake iris, and even economic downturns when the cost of coastal home construction deters development of their habitat, stay the hand of destruction. But for these human actions and inactions, the dwarf lake iris might be far closer to extinction.

While the choice of Michigan's state wildflower appears settled, controversy over the state bird persists. It, too, is instructive on the subject of what's wild. First designated by the legislature in 1929 after a vote of schoolchildren organized by Edith Munger of the Michigan Audubon Society, the robin has reigned despite increasing dissatisfaction in some quarters. The late Glen Sheppard, editor of the *North Woods Call*, intermittently campaigned for the replacement of the robin with the chickadee. The robin was a fair-weather friend, he said, while the chickadee remained in Michigan throughout the winter.

A third bird had its lobbyists, too. The chickadee is found across much of the United States and is already the official state bird of Maine and Massachusetts. Only one bird claims Michigan as its principal habitat—the Kirtland's warbler.

Ninety-eight percent of this little (average 0.55-ounce) yellow-breasted bird's world population nests in Michigan in spring and summer. It came close to extinction in the early 1970s and mid-1980s, when only 167 pairs were counted in the breeding area of north-central lower Michigan. Restoration was simple but not easy. Humans had to intervene, conducting prescribed burns and logging to allow for regeneration of the small jack pine that warblers need for nesting habitat. The cycle of burning and replanting mimics the pre-European cycle of fire and regeneration that ended when forest managers began suppressing forest fire.[‡] In 2019, the estimated Michigan breeding population was 2,300 pairs, double the recovery goal needed to remove the bird from Endangered Species Act listing.

The bird was back—not purely because of a "natural" process, but because humans cared enough to spend money and sweat protecting it. The species would make a fitting state symbol, even if it winters in the Bahamas.

[‡]   Control of parasitic brown-headed cowbirds has also played an important role in recovery of the Kirtland's warbler. The birds lay eggs in Kirtland's nest, and the warblers hatch and raise the offspring as if their own species. Kirtland's protectors in and out of government have placed cowbird traps in the jack pine, and in combination with forest growth in the area, which cowbirds don't favor, the amount of predation has dramatically declined.

Jones

We were out for a country ride to catch some air on a June evening of soggy air and stagnant heat. Passing between a couple of farms, we heard the screeching of a wounded animal. I stopped the car and we walked to the ditch, and looked down. Two tiny puppies writhed in it.

We took the little ones home, eventually adopting the yellow one and finding a friend to take the black. We named him Jones.

We knew he would be big a few weeks before it started to happen because his paws were elephantine even when his body had barely grown. Sure enough, he matured at perhaps forty pounds.

His quirks were endearing. At the lake, he chased the waves laterally as they broke along the sand, never quite catching up. When I shoveled snow, he leaped high in the air to snap at it.

Jones was one of the few dogs I've ever known who would remain by you even when off leash. His eyes were attentive to whoever his human leader was. He wanted to please—and protect. He assumed the guard position, but benignly, when a stranger walked up to us in the woods.

Even more than the usual dog, Jones was an enthusiast of treats. He received way too many, especially from me. Little imitation hot dogs, rawhides, pig's hooves (can't believe I ever did that), and of course everything he could beg from meals or snatch from the kitchen counter. A loaf of fresh-baked bread, for example.

Jones's simple nature never soured. He loved living.

Politics and Fish

S port fish are recreation, food, money, jobs—and politics.

In 1970, scientists detected concentrations of toxic mercury in forty-two fish from Lake St. Clair, a junior Great Lake halfway between Lakes Huron and Erie. The concentrations were twelve to sixteen times higher than the informal public health standard, and almost comparable to mercury levels in fish that had caused death or deformity to 111 people who had consumed tainted fish in Minamata, Japan, in 1968. This—and public fear—prompted both the Ontario provincial government and Michigan's state government to impose emergency shutdown orders on commercial and sport fishing in St. Clair. It was not clear Michigan Governor William Milliken had the authority to halt fishing, but front-page headlines created political pressure to clamp down on yet another toxin, prompting him to act after initial hesitation.*

Once the industrial sources of mercury feeding the lake and connecting waters were controlled, and the emergency subsided, state officials saw they had a new problem to address. Fish contaminants weren't just going to drain away. Many

---

* In 1965 and 1966, public concern about the pesticide dieldrin peaked; in 1969, Michigan became the first state to cancel most uses of DDT.

contaminants were persistent, taking a long time to break down. And surely more would be discovered. What could Michigan's public health experts do to guide the public safely through a poisonous mix of fish contaminants?

Out of necessity, thus, was born Michigan's sport fish consumption advisory. Reflecting the latest detected contaminant levels and the science of risk assessment, the advisories attempted to balance concern about eating pollution with the benefits of eating protein. The advisory would recommend amounts and sizes of fish that could be eaten safely by various subgroups—women of child-bearing age, children, and all others. That was the design, at least. In practice, the advisory would be criticized and politicized. When, late each winter, the state Department of Public Health issued the advisory, constituencies and journalists inevitably viewed it as a scorecard. Was pollution growing or shrinking based on the number of statewide or local advisories? What did this say about the environmental policies of the governor in charge? Was the department too conservative or too lax in protecting the public from the health effects of toxic chemicals? That is, was it fulfilling its public health mission, or trying not to give a black eye to the economically important sport fishing sector—the anglers, the bait shops, fishing gear retailers, the local tourism-dependent businesses, and more that would suffer if fishing was seen as risky to health?

When I began participating in Michigan's environmental policy arena in late 1982, the sensational new fish contaminant of concern was a class of chemicals called dioxins. Often the unintentional byproduct of burning or chemical manufacturing, dioxins at the time were characterized as among the most potent toxins known to science. Laboratory animal studies linked them to reproductive and developmental harm and cancers.

And Michigan was at the heart of dioxin country.

Located in Midland, Michigan, the Dow Chemical Company was founded in 1897 to capitalize on the area's extensive brine deposits. Chemist Henry Dow pioneered a process for extracting bromine from the brine, making possible an array of chemicals useful as building blocks for household products—and lethal war materials, including tear gas in World War I and napalm and Agent Orange during the Vietnam War. Dow grew into a corporate behemoth, adding plastic to its portfolio and ringing up billions in sales by the early 1970s.

But the corporation's hostility to government regulation was undeniable, and its plant site conditions inscrutable. After more than seventy-five years on the Midland property, Dow's estate was suspected to be a chemical brew. But no one knew. The company jealously guarded any data beyond the minimum it was required to report to government.

Dioxin was top of mind in 1983 because of the highly publicized evacuation of Times Beach, Missouri, in February. A waste oil hauler had been hired to take waste dioxins generated by the manufacturing of Agent Orange at a chemical plant in Verona, Missouri, mix them with oil and spread the substance on roads as a dust suppressant. Children and animals fell ill at one site in 1971, but no effective action resulted until testing revealed dioxin levels three hundred times higher than considered safe. In 1983, the federal government bought out occupants of eight hundred houses and thirty businesses, effectively shutting down the community permanently. The public was paying attention. When the word "dioxin" began to appear in news reports in association with Midland, journalists poured into Michigan looking for scoops. Legislators sought attention by proposing laws to make it a felony to discharge dioxins into the environment. And the health department toughened its advisory for the Tittabawassee River and Saginaw Bay, into which Dow's waste flowed.

That's not to say that the professionals devising the annual advisory were convinced that most Michiganders needed to worry about fish contaminants. The old guard in the Department of Public Health thought the risk was overblown. Several even conducted an experiment on themselves, eating large numbers of fish laced with PCB and measuring levels of the chemical in their bodies. They detected higher levels of PCBs in their blood but, they concluded, no adverse effects on themselves.

The same old guard was deeply skeptical when two researchers at Wayne State University, Sandra and Joseph Jacobson, authored science papers concluding that children of women who ate significant amounts of PCB-contaminated fish displayed subtle neurological differences from other children. Even when their research was replicated, suggesting a loss of IQ points among some children exposed in utero to PCBs, they were unconvinced. But the old guard was unable to soften the advisories.

I contributed to the checkered history of Michigan fish consumption advisories in 1986. That January, the Department of Public Health announced the good news "that fish from Michigan lakes and streams are getting safer to eat," as the *Detroit Free Press* reported in a front-page story. The department was cancelling advisories for game fish on five of seven rivers whose fish had been deemed unsafe to eat in 1985. One of the liberated streams was Dow Chemical's Tittabawassee.

A spokesperson for Dow called it great news, adding, "We feel the dioxin issue is past its peak."

Stunned by the apparent sudden drop in contaminant levels in those rivers, environmental advocates like Mark Van Putten, director of the Ann Arbor–based Great Lakes Natural Resources Center of the National Wildlife Association, contacted me to see what the governor would or could do. I was as astonished as Van Putten was, and told a reporter it was probably premature to remove the advisories. The reporter interpreted this as meaning, "Blanchard may renew warnings."

I had spoken out of turn, failing to consult the appropriate people in the office, least of all the governor. I had also not been consulted about the eagerness of our office to claim credit for the improvement, and imply that it had to do with the governor's environmental program.

So, after a short period of review that actually amounted to an effort to marshal the data to reaffirm the advisory cancellation, the Department of Public Health went ahead as originally planned. My boss explained, "I don't think it's wise for the governor ... to be issuing fish advisory announcements." He added, "We're going to leave that to the scientific community."

I had been spanked.

In 1996, Michigan Governor John Engler decided it was wise for the governor to be issuing fish advisory announcements. He intervened politically in the process of developing the advisory. Hoping to generate positive environmental news, Engler overrode the professional judgment of his public health professionals and ordered them to cancel an advisory that cautioned against eating large Lake Michigan salmon because of dioxin and PCBs. The resulting Engler news release crowed, "For the first time in 25 years, there is no restriction on eating salmon caught in Michigan's waters of the Great Lakes ... the overall trend of declining contaminant levels in Great Lakes fish continues."

Both the process and the message infuriated environmental advocates. Other Great Lakes states were not loosening their advisories. The brazen pressure from the Engler staff to report improvement in dioxin levels in the face of the data was unprecedented. The U.S. Environmental Protection Agency was also displeased. EPA mailed a more protective advisory to over a million Michigan fishing license holders. After a year of skirmishing with the feds, Engler relented. News coverage stressing the risk of dioxin and PCB consumption by women of child-bearing age and young children had the potential to embarrass the governor as the election year of 1998 approached.

But EPA's action in mailing the advisory reinforced a question that had puzzled everyone involved in the advisory process: did anyone actually read the advisory documents, including a detailed fishing guide accompanying the annual fishing license? There were reasons to think not. Anecdotal evidence suggested most anglers dismissed the warnings as based on exaggerated fears and faulty science. I heard a fair number of middle-aged fishermen scoff at the advice. "I've been eating these fish all my life and I'm fine," was one refrain. Another was the flip side: years of eating contaminated fish could not be undone by choosing now to shun fish loaded with dioxins, PCBs, or testified.

At least these people could choose. But what about people who fished for subsistence, not for sport? Researchers believed there were thousands of them, maybe tens of thousands, many unlicensed. They were not likely even to be aware of river-specific advisories. But because they depended on river-caught fish as a cheap source of protein, they and their families might eat far more fish, and be far more exposed to contaminants, than the typical sport angler on whose habits the advisory assumptions were based. The community of subsistence anglers was also thought to contain a disproportionate number of low-income people and people of color.

It was not until the 1990s that Michigan public health officials recognized their fish consumption message was not reaching most of the people whose well-being was most at risk. They experimented with signage along heavily fished rivers, handed out streamlined brochures and fact sheets to anglers, and sponsored fish cleaning demonstrations at river events. Still, they were able to reach only a fraction of the estimated population of subsistence anglers who fished for themselves and their families.

Fish consumption advisories have unique implications for the Indigenous peoples of the Great Lakes. Fish are a staple of their traditional diet. By one estimate, this results in a toxic exposure for the Indigenous between two and thirteen times the rest of the Great Lakes population. Advice to limit fish consumption that comes from state and federal agencies has sometimes been greeted with skepticism; Michigan's Great Lakes tribes won recognition of their treaty fishing rights only after fighting the same governments in court for years.

The only solution that will unite all anglers is the elimination of toxic pollution in fish. But because the contaminants of most health concern don't break down rapidly, they will remain in Great Lakes fish for decades at least. Meanwhile, new contaminants are appearing. In 2021, Wisconsin and Michigan issued advisories to limit consumption of Lake Superior smelt to one meal per month because of PFAS (per- and polyfluoroalkyl substances)—so-called "forever chemicals" that have been used in a wide variety of products.

Fish advisories may or may not be good indicators of the effectiveness of pollution control programs, but the growing list of contaminants in fish makes aquatic life the best indicator of their failure to protect us in the present, let alone right the mistakes of the past.

Spayed and Neutered

've never had a good watchdog, but I've worked for one.

Most of the dogs in my life were more likely to greet and kiss and beg to be petted by a home invader than they were to repel one. I can't hold it against them. They all had other virtues.

So did the watchdog on whose staff I served. The International Joint Commission (IJC), an organization established by a 1909 treaty between Canada and the United States, has, among many other things, the job of monitoring progress made by the two federal governments in protecting the Great Lakes.* That responsibility falls on the commission through a binational water quality agreement signed in 1972 and last updated in 2012. In this sphere, IJC is a watchdog agency, charged with taking an independent look at trends in Great Lakes water quality, the job the governments are doing to improve that quality, and issuing the equivalent of a report card every three years.

---

* The IJC's water quantity role spans the entire 5,000-mile boundary between the United States and Canada, 40 percent of which is water. The IJC rules upon applications for approval of projects affecting boundary or transboundary waters (dams, diversions, and water levels) and may regulate the operation of the projects.

But how independent can a watchdog be when an intruder provides his or her food supply?

That has always been the tension between the IJC's role on paper and its role in the real world of government and politics. Speak too sharply of the failure of governments to improve the health of the Great Lakes, and they may cut IJC's funding. Tone down your judgments, and the IJC will lose credibility with the public.

I've had a chance to see the conflict from both inside and outside of the IJC—outside from 1982 to 2010, and inside as a staff member from 2011 to 2016. During that time, the IJC swung from being an unwelcome critic of the governments to—well, their lapdog.

The watchdog years spanned roughly 1988 to 1994, and 2010 to 2016. Setting in motion the first of those was an unlikely force, a conservative Republican named Gordon Durnil of Indiana. Appointed by President George H. W. Bush, a reward for leadership and fundraising success in the Indiana Republican Party, he brandished a resume that contained no evidence of radicalism. But in 1991, as chair of the U.S. section of the IJC, he stirred up industrial rage and environmentalist praise by putting the commission on record as calling for the phaseout and sunset of chlorinated compounds. This is a bigger deal than it sounds.

The introduction of chlorine into organic compounds has produced some of the most useful products in commerce, and some of the most accursed problems. Chlorination has yielded industrial degreasers, pesticides, fire retardants, and pharmaceuticals. It has also fouled the environment with long-lasting toxic chemicals such as PCBs, DDT, and dioxins. In the Great Lakes system, the latter have been linked to disease in humans as well as fish and wildlife.

The IJC had turned its attention to chlorine because, it seemed, virtually every problem chemical affecting the people and wildlife of the Great Lakes was a chlorine compound. As problems with one chemical troubled the ecosystem, governments responded with bans or strict controls. The replacements often had similar or worse effects. Society, Durnil warned, was chasing individual chemicals when a whole class should be indicted. He was particularly troubled by the hormone-mimicking and endocrine-disrupting properties associated with chlorinated compounds: reduced male sperm counts, fertility problems among young couples, skyrocketing breast cancer rates, abortion of damaged fetuses, and feminization of wildlife.

Durnil brought to the subject matter of Great Lakes pollution a fresh eye—and, the industrial sector thought, a naivete that explained why he didn't know what he was talking about. Regardless, listening to scientists he trusted, he persuaded the other five IJC commissioners to support a call for the "sunsetting" of most chlorine compounds in commerce.

Tired of fighting on a chemical-by-chemical basis and falling farther and farther behind, environmentalists seized on this recommendation. Now working outside of government and free to act on personal belief, I was one of them. I had seen and heard of enough human suffering from exposure to chlorinated compounds.

A horrified industrial community was briefly caught off guard. They had considered the IJC powerless (it had no authority to implement its recommendations) and not likely to rock the boat with conservatives in charge of the U.S. side. But the IJC had a bully pulpit with its highly visible, periodic Great Lakes reports, which interested journalists looking for stories about toxic substances. Soon, the sunsetting idea had currency with some policymakers and elements of the public.

The industry sector prepared testimony to oppose the proposed ban at the 1993 IJC public biennial Great Lakes meeting in Windsor. Environmentalists prepared their own—and more. Their enthusiasm was high. Finally, someone in government had seen the twilight falling over the Great Lakes and her people—the IJC, shattering the timid hesitancy of the government bureaucracies. Activists from across the entire watershed hopped buses, cars, trains, and planes to attend the biennial meeting.

Showing up in Windsor, I was astonished to see a crowd of what would be estimated as 1,900 swarming a large meeting room just across the street from the south bank of the Detroit River, with the skyline of Detroit prominent on the other side. Two kinds of energy animated the participants—excitement among the environmentalists, dread and controlled anger among the industrial crowd. As the comment period began, jeers and shouts greeted the industrialists who spoke.

Mel Visser, an environmental manager at the Kalamazoo-based chemical manufacturer Upjohn Corporation, was among those from industry who offered comments to the commissioners. Mel, who would later become a good friend of mine, remembered the experience this way:

I had just gotten into my talk when I saw something moving in from the left and approaching the aisle directly below me. I looked to see a hissing activist costumed as a cross-beaked cormorant.[†] My eyes must have bugged out and the crowd had

---

† Dioxin pollution was blamed by some scientists as a cause of physical defects in Great Lakes cormorants.

a good laugh. I looked down at my notes and continued talking, but no way was I going to hide from this circus. I looked up to see a flurry of hands raising signs calling me a killer, hack, liar, and whatever. I ducked into my notes again. Next time up I spotted a Chlorine Council staffer who said she would be there if I needed a friendly face. I sure did and was comforted by her warm smile and thumbs up. The flow of cold sweat stopped dripping from my knees. Looking at the back of the crowd I saw a bedsheet unfurled. I finished talking and received polite applause from the industry representatives scattered about the front seats, hisses from the cormorant, and a dull murmur from the crowd. Suddenly the crowd broke out in cheers as the bedsheet covered with messages of our plant's emissions, violations, and speculated sins of the environment flew by.

Meanwhile, I was part of a group preparing to unfurl a different banner. Standing behind the commissioners' seats, perhaps thirty of us spread out a Great Lakes health banner. Individual panels contributed by different communities told in colorful ways of their wish for clean Great Lakes, and their outrage about industrial fouling.

The demeanor of the environmentalists—the rudeness, disrespect, and hostility shown to the opponents of a chlorine ban—appalled me. But I put that aside in deference to what I regarded as the bigger offense, the poisoning of Michigan communities. I was proud to hold that banner.

That turned out to be the peak of the citizen movement to prevent further contamination through a chlorine phaseout. The Chlorine Council may have lost the battle in Windsor, but it won the war in Washington. Durnil left the IJC when the Clinton Administration replaced him in 1994, going on to author the book *The Making of a Conservative Environmentalist*. The new U.S. team appointed by Clinton heard from some key members of Congress that they would whack at IJC's budget if it did not pull back on the chlorine ban and its demonization of industry. The commission complied. And over the next few years, the public constituency the IJC had attracted faded away. The audiences at the biennial public meetings shrank by 95 percent.[‡]

[‡] The IJC did make a difference on another recommendation in the same biennial report. The IJC recommended that the Canadian and U.S. governments designate Lake Superior as a "zero discharge demonstration area" where no end-of-pipe source discharge of any persistent toxic chemical will be permitted. The two governments accepted this challenge and launched a program to take it on. Thirty years later, they had achieved reductions of as much as 80 percent for the nine pollutants selected, but they were far from the goal of zero.

For more than a decade afterward, the IJC conducted Great Lakes studies and issued reports but rocked no boats. There was no talk of strict regulation of toxic chemicals to restore Great Lakes water quality. But in 2010, an appointee of President Obama, former Michigan State Senator Lana Pollack, took over the U.S. section.

Lana and I went back to the 1980s, when she had won my admiration for her fearless approach to legislating. She was not afraid to propose legislation that seemed outlandish to some but was in fact ahead of its time. Nor was she afraid to challenge her legislative colleagues, 95 percent of whom were male when she took office in 1983. One of my favorite Lana Pollack stories has to do with a sidebar meeting on the senate floor. One of the good old boy senators, whom Lana knew had made sexually coarse comments about her, casually put his hand on her shoulder. She stared at him and said, "Take your hand off me!"

The group fell silent. The surprised senator mumbled an uncertain, "What?"

Lana said, "You heard me. Don't you ever touch me again."

Lana put to work her combination of policy brain, persistence, drive—and diplomacy when needed—on the IJC. While maintaining cordial relations with representatives of the Canadian and U.S. governments, she carved out an independent role for the commission. External constituencies began to take the IJC seriously again.

One successful project she pushed forward was a plan to attack the disturbing problem of algae blooms in western Lake Erie. In 1966, my family had driven from our Dearborn home to Point Pelee National Park in Ontario for a day of swimming and picnicking. Arriving, we found a sickening pea-green soup in which no nine-year-old was going to bathe. Not long after, the IJC issued a study with recommendations on how to restore some sort of water quality to the western basin of Erie by reducing phosphorus in laundry soaps and sewage discharges. That, in turn, led to the 1972 Great Lakes Water Quality Agreement and the start of a dramatic recovery in Erie.

But around the year 2000, the lake's algae blooms roared back, expanding in some years to suffocate large swaths of the western basin. Under Lana's lead, the IJC published a 2014 report calling for a 40 percent reduction in phosphorus pollution entering the lake, with a focus on the largely untouched agricultural sector, whose fertilizers and animal wastes were fueling the algae. The 40 percent figure became the touchstone for agreements among the western basin's governments, including Michigan, although in 2021 they were far from achieving the goal. And the report's most important recommendation, that governments get serious and control nutrients from farms, has gotten nowhere. The politics are too tough.

The tension inherent in serving as a watchdog while receiving sustenance from the watched continues. There may be no way to get around it, unless governments have enough courage and confidence to endow permanently an independent evaluator of Great Lakes progress. The province of Ontario tried, empowering an independent environmental commissioner from 1994 to 2019. Premier Doug Ford abolished it in 2019.

Watchdogs are generally not welcome in the political process. They bark too much at election time.

Dude

A rescue dog, Dude had an outlaw's spirit. When I met him, I couldn't take my eyes off him. Was he really a dog? He had the reddish-brown coat of a fox, and his eyes appeared cagey like a fox's.

The first time I walked him, he made a break for freedom and almost succeeded, but I grabbed his hind end. He didn't wriggle. He looked at me with what looked like a grin. "Can't blame a guy for trying," he seemed to say.

Attempted escape was his favorite pastime, second only to eating. I learned after several prison breaks not to open the door when he was within ten feet of it. He had the speed of a track star. Once he was gone the better part of a summer day, and I despaired of seeing him again. Just before dusk, I heard his coughing bark outside the back door. I turned on the light to see a red dog turned green. Prickers covered his face and the front half of his body. He attempted a rueful smile but was panting with exhaustion. I spent almost an hour combing and plucking the damn things out of his fur. He closed his eyes in sheer enjoyment. My attending to him, he seemed to think, was his due.

I had no idea how old Dude was when I met him, but he was older than I thought. In his third winter after rescue, he slowed noticeably. He moved more slowly, gingerly, and slept far more. By March he had lost his freedom of movement.

I carried him outdoors to relieve himself. The old rebel gave me quick kisses. When I massaged his back, he made appreciative old man sounds. I often spent a half hour at a time kneading his back.

When Dude passed, I wept, but remembering Dude now, I imagine a grin creasing his face. It consoles me to think that in escaping from this Earth, he found a new place to romp unhindered.

Toxic Shock

I t started with a peculiar phenomenon in my left foot. Occasionally, and unpre-
dictably, it would tighten, cramp and then curl up painfully. Walking was nearly
impossible. Only by turning my foot on its left side could I move, and even then,
painfully and slowly. It happened once when I was walking a city block from
home. It took me fifteen minutes to stagger a distance I usually traveled in one.

About a year later, I was driving the interstate well after dark when fear pulsed
through me. The slight curve in the road, taken at seventy miles per hour, left me
looking into a black abyss. I couldn't see the pavement ahead. I slowed to fifty-five,
still feeling uneasy.

A few months on, I fumbled with the seat belt each time I got in the car.
Matching the key to the ignition was irritatingly difficult. It sometimes took a
dozen tries and five minutes to get it right. When accompanied by passengers, I
grew flustered and apologetic.

Next came the drooling. Sitting at my desk, driving, walking—it didn't matter.
I would suddenly feel saliva oozing out of the corners of my mouth. Fortunately,
my beard hid it from others most of the time—but not all. Once, in a meeting,
my boss politely signaled me to wipe some of the moisture away from my mouth.

Eating sometimes resulted in embarrassment. Increasingly, I choked on food. Large pieces of chewed bread, crackers, even fruit lodged in the back of my throat. Spasms of coughing followed, and often, a trip to the nearest faucet to gulp down several glasses of water.

I enjoy writing, but it seemed as though it became a chore overnight. I didn't have enough pressure in my fingers to drive the keystrokes on my computer. Often, I had to resort to a technique I'd used thirty years before as a reporter when my fingers lacked the muscle to influence the keyboard on a conventional typewriter. I used my right index finger for everything. It was clumsy, time-consuming, and frustrating. My mind far outraced my finger, especially when numerous missed keys slowed me down. I began to worry whether writing itself would become impossible.

The most difficult task of all, suddenly, was buttoning my shirt and tying a tie. I cursed in frustration as I struggled to match button and buttonhole. After a while this could take up to half an hour. A tie could take another ten minutes. Thus, for an evening ceremony in Grand Rapids that began at 7 p.m., I began dressing at 5:45—and was almost late.

Something was wrong, clearly. I didn't want to find out what. A brain tumor or stroke were the two possibilities that occurred to me. I decided I'd rather not know.

Two friends were not in the same depth of denial. They insisted that I see a neurologist. Months after they made the suggestion, I finally acted. After answering the neurologist's questions, I stood up and walked down the hall and back. She asked me to sit down and said that without doubt, I had Parkinson's disease.

My first reaction was relief. Sure, Parkinson's is a degenerative disease with no cure—but it sure beat a brain tumor or a stroke. The neurologist suggested a few simple therapies: intense aerobic exercise, physical therapy, consistent sleep, and a healthy diet. When she asked whether I drank coffee, I shuddered. "Don't tell me I have to give it up," I said, ready to plead for my cherished morning ritual. She smiled and said that something to the effect that caffeine countered the loss of dopamine that figured in Parkinson's. She prescribed the go-to pharmaceutical for Parkinson's, Sinemet.

Within two weeks of beginning the medication my symptoms eased, but not all and not completely, any one of them. Still, when I next saw the neurologist, I almost fell to my knees in gratitude. My life was 95 percent of what it had been before Parkinson's began to creep up on me. I didn't take the improvement for granted.

Naturally, I wondered where the disease came from. My brother Jack, who had done yeoman's work researching the family history, had found no traces of Parkinson's through the recent generations. Which, I decided, meant one of two things—random chance or environmental causes. The human mind rejects randomness out of hand, despite the obvious fact that it is a sculptor of human destiny. So, I turned to environmental causes in the broadest sense—not just the air and water I'd been working to protect, but anything external to the body.

Or at least I tried. I consulted Parkinson's support groups, scientific literature, and my neurologist, who named many potential nonhereditary triggers, but none any more likely than the others. I turned back to the matter with which I was familiar—the toxic chemicals associated with so much of our commerce.

I reflected on an analysis of my blood that had been performed out of academic interest in 1989. One of the government programs I supervised was a long-term study of human health effects arising from exposure to PBB, the flame retardant. A 1973 industrial accident mixed PBB with cattle feed, and the chemical penetrated the Michigan food chain, resulting in almost universal human exposure and detectable levels of PBB in most Michigan residents who were tested. I was no exception. In fact, it is my memory that my blood had yielded a surprisingly high concentration of PBB. It made little sense. I hadn't lived or worked on the most affected farms; the farm families, raising affected livestock and poultry, had paid a significant but as yet unquantifiable price for the accident. That was the whole purpose of the long-term study: to focus on the most vulnerable. The only explanation I could conceive for my relatively high PBB concentration was that as a sixteen-year-old in 1973, I had consumed mammoth quantities of milk and meat, especially hamburgers. But I wasn't unique in that regard.

I searched the online scientific literature periodically. Four years after my diagnosis and with the help of Google, I finally found mention of a possible PBB-Parkinson's link. It was intriguing. Deriving serum samples from the Michigan cohort tracked by the program I had been administering in 1989, three Howard University researchers published a paper in February 2019 that concluded:

Metabolic alterations were correlated with PBB-153 and PCB-153 in both generations of participants, and included changes in pathways related to catecholamine
metabolism, cellular respiration, essential fatty acids, lipids and polyamine
metabolism. These pathways were consistent with pathophysiological changes

observed in neurodegenerative disease and included previously identified metabolomic markers of Parkinson's disease.[*]

Science in general does not point at smoking guns. This was just one of many studies of health markers potentially linked to PBB exposure. Many searched for and some found associations with other health effects, including forms of cancer in women. But even they did not prove cause and effect. It would take years and many studies to build support for the hypothesis of a Parkinson's connection, if it could be supported. The paper I found dealt with the farm families and offspring, who had a profoundly greater exposure than I had had.

PBB is not the only synthetic chemical that has been associated with Parkinson's. The authors of *Ending Parkinson's Disease: A Prescription for Action*, published in 2020, say the prevalence of Parkinson's has risen in tandem with the use of pesticides, industrial solvents, and degreasing agents in countries throughout the world.[†] An example is TCE, the widely used industrial solvent that has contaminated three hundred known locations in Michigan—and, the authors say, nearly everyone in the United States has been exposed to it in one way or another.

The growth in numbers and use of toxic substances and exposure to their wastes and byproducts, say the authors of *Ending Parkinson's*, is contributing to a global pandemic of the disease. Global prevalence rates, adjusted for age, soared 22 percent in the quarter century leading up to 2020.

I had cause, now, to think of my life's experience with toxic chemicals. I couldn't remember even hearing the word until 1981 or 1982, when there was news about "toxic shock syndrome" affecting women who used super-absorbent tampons. An overwhelming release of toxins from the tampons was discovered to drive blood pressure down suddenly to dangerous levels, in some cases leading to death. Ultimately, manufacturers were required to pull the products from store shelves.

---

[*]   Douglas I. Walker, M. Elizabeth Marder, Yukiko Yano, Metrecia Terrell, Yongliang Liang, Dana Boyd Barr, Gary W. Miller, Dean P. Jones, Michele Marcus, and Kurt D. Pennell, "Multigenerational Metabolic Profiling in the Michigan PBB Registry," *Environmental Research* 172 (2019): 182–93, https://doi.org/10.1016/j.envres.2019.02.018.

[†]   Ray Dorsey, Todd Sherer, Michael Okun, and Bastiaan R. Bloem, *Ending Parkinson's Disease: A Prescription for Action* (New York: Public Affairs, 2020).

I had managed to avoid taking notice in the late 1970s of the earliest and one of the most notorious toxic waste disasters, one affecting residents of a neighborhood known as Love Canal near Niagara Falls, New York. Chemicals oozing to the land surface and into basements in the neighborhood were waste disposed of by Hooker Chemical Company years before. The company had buried the waste and sold off the land for development. The mess infuriated and radicalized residents of the Love Canal area, who feared for their own and their children's health. Several years of pressure on local, state, and federal officials ultimately led to a buyout of many homeowners who wanted to leave, and to the disposal of the wastes at a licensed location. Love Canal was the most publicized of many abandoned toxic waste sites that would be found across the nation by the early 1980s.

Still, I was aware that the word "toxic" was inflammatory. It scared people. So, working for Congressional candidate Bob Carr in his 1982 campaign, I inserted the word into a news release. The incumbent opponent had voted against applying strict standards for hazardous waste management to smaller businesses. The release branded him a "toxic Congressman." While demagogic and emotionally satisfying in the moment (and regretted later), the news release attracted little attention.

By the mid-1980s, working for a governor of a state convulsed by waste, landfill, and incinerator controversies, I was on a first-name basis with all things toxic. It seemed every explosive environmental issue featured alphabet soup—PCBs, DDT, TCE, PBB, and so forth. "Ethyl methyl bad stuff" was the generic nickname sarcastically applied by one state official to the parade of chemicals.

After a while, it was impossible for me to think of environmental issues as primarily the conservation of lands and waters and the reduction of well-known pollutants like lead. Chemical controversies engulfed me, state agencies, other state governments and the EPA. The Michigan Department of Natural Resources inventoried the state and identified thousands of potentially contaminated areas, from old dumps to abandoned factories and riverbeds lacquered with industrial runoff from upstream. Like Americans in general, I was becoming aware that we had been bathing ourselves in toxins whose risks we ill understood. "Invasion" was a better word for it—or trespass. We had not knowingly authorized this assault on our bodies. No one had ever communicated that we even had a choice to make. The lack of regulation of many of these chemicals created a Wild West of commerce where manufacturers policed themselves—very little.

Every toxic chemical newly detected in fish and wildlife, food, soil, air, and indoors was front-page news in the 1980s. Screaming headlines speculated on grave human health risks. "Toxic" became an adjective that boosted ratings or subscriptions. In turn, concerns the coverage raised often led to useful policy actions, including immediate bans or phaseouts of the chemical offenders and cleanup of the most offending residual contamination.

This wasn't all to the good. Occasionally, journalists would break stories of dangerous compounds that turned out to be minor problems. That could drive irrational policies and discredit concern about the next chemical sensation. Too often, reporters and environmental groups would collaborate in fanning the flames.

But the human limbic system can absorb shocks only so long before becoming acclimated. This is a natural—you could say a wild—response. And we are a species that responds to novelty. By the end of the 1980s, the menace of toxic chemicals was receding as a public concern. That was and is a pity. The systemic reforms needed to protect human health and ecological security, especially a cradle-to-grave management system for all chemicals, including those about to be introduced to the market, never materialized. Chemical companies and associations were gratified. By fighting a rearguard action on each of the troublesome chemicals detected at levels of concern in the 1980s, they had prevented the focus from shifting to American chemical policy.

Which is why new problem chemicals replaced the old. As just one example, when the United States banned PBB as a fire retardant following Michigan's disaster, chemical makers and users switched to PBDEs. These substitutes were soon found to cause their own health and environmental problems. They built up in the human body and were only slowly shed. In the early 2000s, EPA and the states banned or phased out the most commonly used PBDEs. But no mechanism was in place to evaluate automatically the substitute for PBDEs. Our society had learned little. We were repeating our mistakes, jeopardizing the health of millions. Collectively, we were numb.

The work goes on. Many talented and brilliant environmental advocates continue to work on chemical policy. But it is hard to see how they will make a breakthrough in the American political process without some kind of revolution in the campaign finance and election system.

This is all academic to my body. It doesn't care about policy. It won't be rid of Parkinson's by a new discovery of effective treatment. There simply isn't enough time. In the end, knowing which, if any toxic chemical triggered the disease is impossible. I will just have to accept my fate. So many others have done so before, in more difficult circumstances. They've suffered cancer, or reproductive impairment, or lost IQ points. The human body didn't evolve to handle the thousands of toxic chemicals in commerce. This intrusion on the natural ecosystem of the human organism will persist for generations.

Suckers

I t was December 1989. Something was clogging the Lake Erie drinking water intake of the city of Monroe, interrupting the flow to city residents. Two days would pass before Monroe was able to supply all of its citizens with drinking water again. What the heck was going on?

An exotic species known as the zebra mussel, *Dreissena polymorpha*, a European mollusk, had found the Great Lakes a welcoming new home. Stowing away in the ballast water of a commercial vessel conducting cross-Atlantic trade, the mussels had disembarked in the lakes and, with no natural predators, had rapidly proliferated.* And they had found surfaces to which they could cling.

Although the interruption of Monroe's public drinking water supply was the first real alert to the general public that a new pest was in town, scientists had already been aware of the invaders. They had discovered the mussels in Lake St. Clair in 1988. But no one had predicted the explosion of zebra mussel populations in such a short time.† Soon the species would become the headliner for a Great

---

* Zebra mussels are native to the Black, Caspian, and Azov Seas.

† It turned out that each female zebra mussel could produce as many as a million eggs annually. They were soon found at a density of as much as 100,000 per square meter, attaching themselves to hard surfaces—human made structures and native mussels, whom they starved, among other things.

Lakes problem reaching back into the 1800s—the intentional and unintentional introduction of non-native aquatic organisms.

It was not the first time that a destructive non-native species had caused such severe disruption that governments were forced to react. In the 1940s and 1950s, the monstrous-looking sea lamprey, equipped with a large mouth containing numerous small teeth, had attacked Great Lakes fish with such voraciousness, sucking the lifeblood out of lake trout and other species, that the United States and Canada had signed the 1955 Great Lakes Fishery Convention to launch a counterattack.

I became familiar with the war on lamprey as a member of the Great Lakes Fishery Commission (GLFC), created by the 1955 convention, from 1994 to 2001. At their peak, before the creation of the GLFC, lamprey had killed more than 100 million pounds of Great Lakes fish each year. The commission was charged with controlling the lamprey.

More than forty years into the contest, government and lamprey were stalemated. Treatment of the lamprey with a targeted chemical at a cost of about $20 million annually, paid out of the GLFC budget, held lamprey generally in check. The annual lamprey fish kill had fallen to less than 10 million pounds. But there was no sign, and no likelihood, that humans would ever eradicate the eels from the Great Lakes. Like many other non-natives, the lamprey had multiplied astonishingly after reaching the upper lakes, and then hit an equilibrium where they could be managed, controlled, but not vanquished. Like a person keeping a chronic illness at bay with medication, Great Lakes fishery managers would need, possibly forever, to treat spawning rivers with toxins.

The anti-lamprey war did breed creativity. Experiments showed that underwater barriers could limit passage of adult lamprey upstream into spawning habitat. Less successfully, researchers explored the idea of lamprey birth control—introducing sterile males, who could theoretically outcompete those capable of contributing to reproduction. Policy makers even explored the idea of capturing Great Lakes lamprey and shipping them to European markets, where the animals are considered good eating. In 1996, the Great Lakes Protection Fund awarded Minnesota Sea Grant funding to conduct a two-year study on the overseas market potential for Great Lakes sea lamprey. At the time, lamprey had a potential market value of over $25 per pound in Europe, and the Portuguese expressed an interest in North American lamprey. Unfortunately, Great Lakes lamprey were too loaded with toxic contaminants to be advisable eating for Europeans or any other humans.[‡]

Given the wake-up call of the lamprey invasion, and the consequences of approximately 180 non-native species introductions since European settlement of the Great Lakes watershed by the 1950s, it would have made sense for governmental and scientific Great Lakes experts to be alert to the potential for harm from future non-native migrants. But they either wouldn't or couldn't marshal the will to demand preventive action. Experts had warned in the 1970s that zebra mussels could readily colonize the Great Lakes, but governments had taken no action to stop them. And now the cost to taxpayers, sport fishers, and the shipping industry would be staggering. Estimates of the annual cost of non-native mussels to the Great Lakes economy vary from hundreds of millions of dollars to several billion. The national cost was much higher. The Great Lakes were not the last U.S. stop for zebra mussels. In 2021, they had established themselves in more than six hundred lakes and reservoirs in at least thirty-three states.

One of the first newspaper reports about the impact on Monroe's drinking water intake left until the final paragraph, almost in passing, the consequence of the zebra mussel infestation that would soon prove its most formidable challenge: "The growth of the mussels upsets the food balance in the lake, which could negatively affect salmon, perch, and walleye fisheries."[§]

That would prove true on a large scale. Zebra mussels and their cousins, non-native quagga mussels, consume the micro-organisms on which desirable Great Lakes sport fish feed. This eating habit would contribute to plunging salmon populations in some areas of the lakes and reduced growth for species like walleye. The future of the Great Lakes sport fishery became uncertain.

The onslaught of zebra and quagga mussels was only the newest chapter in the saga of human-introduced, non-native aquatic species in the Great Lakes. Non-natives had reached the Great Lakes system in all manner of ways. In

---

‡ Some on the North American side of the Atlantic did find the lamprey to be good eating. After cutting their heads off, Lars Rudstam, director of the Cornell Biological Field Station in New York, made Lamprey Bordelaise with a wine sauce, spices, and lamprey chunks. The resulting dish, he said, tasted like squid. David Figura, "Eating Sea Lamprey: They're Not Bad to Stomach after You Cut the Head Off," *Syracuse Post-Standard*, April 19, 2013, https://www.syracuse.com/.

§ Tim Jones, "Mussels' Damage Not Limited to Impeding Water Intake Flow," *Detroit Free Press*, December 19, 1989, p. 1B.

addition to hitchhiking in ballast water, they had made it to the lakes in bait, illegal transport, dumping of waste fish, inadvertent transport by recreational boats, swimming up the system through canals—and sometimes through intentional acts.

There is still a need for preventive action to protect the Great Lakes from non-native species. A 2021 study identified 144 additional species, both plant and animal, which had the potential to reproduce in the watershed through natural dispersal, hitchhiking, and intentional release.[¶] The tools for protective action exist. Can governments depart from practices of the past to act in advance of a crisis?

There is also the question of whether the term "invasive" is accurate. After I gave a talk at Macalester College about the risk of Asian carp invasion of the lakes, a Ph.D. contrarian in the audience rose and begged to differ. He observed that humans are a natural part of the global ecosystem, and thus if their actions resulted in new species reaching the Great Lakes, this was simply the result of natural processes. It is a valid point to consider. What is natural and what is not? What is wild and what is not? Are they false dichotomies?

Once, early in my career, a friend and I stood on a Lake Michigan beach, marveling at the sweeping blue carpet of water covering nearly a 180-degree panorama. It was late autumn, and the water was free of vessels. We remarked on how the lake surface, from that vantage point on that day, was exactly what a human observer would have seen 5,000 years before. We agreed it was an aquatic wilderness area, where people were transients.

That was five years before the zebra mussel introduced itself to Monroe and demonstrated that the Great Lakes—both underwater and at the surface—are no wilderness. Before long, the mussels would transform that surface. By filtering particles of phosphorus, they clarified the water, creating the illusion of a cleaner lake when one gazed downward. Rather, such clarity signaled processes at work that few had anticipated, and whose evolution few could predict.

If the surface of the Great Lakes sometimes resembled a "Big Wild," this was an illusion. Human action and inaction had transformed the lakes into a cross between an aquarium and a monumental scientific experiment. Invasive species made it clear that these waters were at best half wild.

[¶] A. D. Davidson, A. J. Tucker, W. L. Chadderton, and C. Weibert, "Development of a Surveillance Species List to Inform Aquatic Invasive Species Management in the Laurentian Great Lakes," *Management of Biological Invasions* 12, no. 2 (2021): 272–93, https://doi.org/10.3391/mbi.2021.12.2.05.

Watershed Living

had the honor of living next to one of the Great Lakes. From 2015 to 2018, I rented a cottage beside Lake Huron just north of the city of Port Huron. Every day I was at home, I awoke knowing it was there, an immense, friendly presence like a whale. In all seasons I often rose to watch the sun rise. I watched night fall over Huron, too. The big water was never far from my thoughts and feelings. I thought of the lake as willingly sharing itself with me and thousands of others each day.

Moving away from the lake saddened me. It was necessary because I took a new job in a city 250 miles away and couldn't afford two rental payments each month. But I was melancholy the day I turned in my cottage keys at the end of September 2018. I took one last trip down to the water, watched my lengthening autumn shadow on the lake's surface, thanked Huron for helping me through a difficult period of life, and said a solemn goodbye.

Of course, in Michigan, no matter where you live, water is no abstraction. A lake, a river, a wetland is always within reach. My new home was an apartment within a ten-minute walk of the western arm of Grand Traverse Bay. It was comforting, but it wasn't the same.

I had been spoiled. Fifty steps had formerly taken me from a cottage to a Great Lake. It wasn't so much the extra effort now involved; it's that the bay was simply not as intimate. I couldn't hear the pounding waves from the apartment. I couldn't see water from my living room. Even touching the water of the bay required crossing a busy divided parkway. The occasions when water now insisted on my attention were few. Like the time in spring when the wind suddenly backed out of the north and blew the breath of the winter-chilled Grand Traverse down my street four blocks away. The air temperature immediately plunged ten degrees.

Still, water bewitches you. Its subtlety as well as its majesty has the power to charm. I settled into my new home and sought to learn about my new watershed.

The major water features of my new habitat were creeks. Walking my dog Fitz, I came across several rivulets traversing the neighborhood so unobtrusively as to near invisibility. I heard one of them before I saw it. Standing on the sidewalk of a densely populated residential neighborhood, I heard a whooshing sound. I looked around. Wind? Traffic? Finally, I spotted a waterway perhaps two feet wide running roughly diagonally through the back yard of a nearby home. I took Fitz around the block to see where it led.

Its destination was a culvert leading under an alley. It simply disappeared. I wasn't ready to give up, however. I walked down the alley in the direction the little creek had been flowing. Sure enough, a few hundred feet east, it emerged into the daylight. It wasn't the same ditched watercourse as above. Here it waved and wiggled through plantings of what looked like native wildflowers and forbs. It was clean and clear.

The emergence was located across the street from the Cowles Cancer Center on the Munson Hospital campus. As I walked through the creek garden, I read signs crediting the agencies and organizations that had spent money and devoted effort to its creation. Another sign invited those in need of peace and reflection to stroll or sit on one of several benches. This was a magic enclave, surrounded by concrete and buildings but restored and living. I accepted the invitation, sitting in the Sunday sun while Fitz rested at my feet.

I wanted to know the name of this creek. That seemed essential to its identity. To know its name, to know where it began and into what waters it emptied was important to me.

I turned to the internet for assistance. A map showed a blue line generally where I thought I had been but offered no name. It did show the creek's progression further east and then south from the garden, and thence again to the east, met by a sister creek.

The map gave the sister a name—Kids Creek. It was a thought-provoking name. Was it a waterbody that had once delighted, or still did delight children? Or was it simply the name of a person who had once lived on it or near it?

I dove further into the internet, on one of those searches that, like a train of thought, can lead to unexpected places and dead ends. Checking out Kids Creek, I found much information, including a summary of the creek "daylighting" as it entered the garden. The project was part of a much bigger campaign to restore Kids Creek, which in turn was part of an even bigger campaign to restore the Great Lakes. And the little brook that had captured my attention? It turned out to be an "unnamed tributary" of Kids Creek. I decided to name it Fitz Creek.

It turns out Kids Creek is a roughly five-mile-long tributary of the Boardman River. From its head upslope south of the city, it snakes under and around busy US-31, never out of earshot of the traffic that roars in the daytime.

Kids Creek's name dates back to 1958 and succeeded the name Asylum Creek, derived from its passage near the grounds of the state mental hospital. As the *Traverse City Record-Eagle* explained about the change from Asylum Creek, "hospital employes [*sic*] feel that this term is little more than a throw-back to the days when there was a great deal of ignorance on the subject of mental illness. Today, the stigma of mental illness has been dropped, along with the word 'asylum' and in its place has come the general realization that mental illness can be treated just as successfully as the normal run of physical ills."* And why Kids Creek?

Because the creek had become "almost a 'way of life' to countless youngsters in the Traverse City area, most of whom fish it because it is easy to reach by bicycle or on foot." That observation gave me a few pangs because it expressed a time when many kids (a) fished and (b) felt, along with their parents, that it was safe to venture beyond the neighborhood without adult supervision.

As I explored the neighborhood, I found that just to the east, the creek was confined by concrete walls and fouled by sediment, oil, grease, and other wastes. This was a far cry from the creek's character early in European settlement days, when, according to the hometown paper, it provided habitat for the exquisite grayling, and even into the mid-1960s, when a healthy brook trout population enjoyed its entire length.

Other tributaries without names bordered the grounds of the old mental hospital, now converted to retail, restaurant, office, and living space and known as the Commons. Completed in 1885, the hospital had once been the proving ground

---

* "Asylum Creek to Become 'Kids Creek,'" Traverse City Record-Eagle, March 15, 1958, p. 1.

for the hypothesis that exposure to the outdoors was a key therapy. The abundant springs and surface water of the site were important assets for the hospital.

Under the hospital's first medical superintendent, Dr. J. D. Munson, the grounds featured an expansive working farm. "The farm operations were an integral part of the hospital complex," the 2009 redevelopment master plan noted, "providing therapeutic employment for able bodied patients and nourishing food for its staff and patients. Farm operations included such livestock as a large beef and dairy cattle herd, horses, hogs, and fowl. Crop operations included apple, peach and cherry orchards, vineyards and berry patches, and a full complement of garden crops, particularly potatoes which were a staple of the institution." But shrinking state budgets and an emphasis on psychiatric drug therapies, family care, and returning patients to the community led to the hospital's closing in 1989. The award-winning resurrection of the buildings and grounds as a hub of commerce followed early in the new century.

On Saturday mornings, Fitz and I typically got up and walked between 8 and 9 a.m. from our living space a block north of the Commons. Well before the hubbub of the day, we strode alongside creeks converted in places to drainage ditches, one such watercourse making a hard-right turn at a street intersection. Yet in other places on the Commons grounds, brooks curled lazily around trees and flowed unhurried to a confluence.

The more I explored with Fitz, the more feeder creeks and trickles I found. To the northwest, a creek paralleling Front Street descended from a slight elevation. One day I saw a lone fish swimming upstream.

The Watershed Center of Grand Traverse Bay had lovingly created the healing garden, removing the creek's concrete ceiling and planting native shrubs and flowers. The project created a quarter mile of meandering stream, eliminated the equivalent of 1.25 football fields of concrete, and established a 27,000-square-foot floodplain.

The project undid what at one time, late in the nineteenth and well into the twentieth century, had been regarded as progress. Officials made decisions that turned natural waterways into rigid drains, which they considered beneficial. The goal in those days was to usher water as fast as possible downstream, and ultimately to the bay.

There's a lot of mending to do. A stream assessment of Kids Creek not far upstream of the former State Hospital, done in 2015 by the Michigan Department of Environmental Quality, was critical of its relatively poor aquatic life. "The substrate was mostly sand and silt with minimal gravel. Large sand deposits were noted and large woody debris in the channel was very embedded. An extensive amount of aquatic macrophytes, including the non-native, invasive curly-leaf pond weed (*Potamogeton crispus*) was in the channel. Overhanging vegetation was moderately available, and all other habitat types were sparse. Recent evidence of channel alteration was observed." The creek joined the state's Clean Water Act "nonattainment" list, meaning it failed to meet water quality standards.

Getting to know each of the tributary streams and Kids Creek was like slowly getting to know new friends. Each had its personality, from loud and gabbling to a gentle whisper; each had its pace, from a big hurry to thinking about getting there someday; and each had its appearance, from clear with a sandy bottom to brown and turbid. And like taking the time to understand people you have just met, focusing on each of these watercourses opens your heart a little. Their idiosyncrasies inspire appreciation, even love.

My second home in the Traverse City region was approximately four miles to the southeast, outside the city limits. Water was again a central feature of my habitat.

I had heard of it and driven by the entrance once, but only after I moved to its periphery did I visit the Miller Creek Nature Reserve. An eighty-eight-acre assemblage of square, rectangular, and triangular pieces of land, the preserve was narrow enough that traffic sounds penetrated most of the time. But after a while they didn't register. The calming sound of flowing water winding in several small brooks became the dominant sensory impression.

The branches of Miller Creek flowed at the base of a ridge running southwest to northeast. In places the ridge had a steep shoulder. Sand and gravel spilled from its side, with the sand piling up at the bottom after heavy rains. It also spilled into the creek.

An old red pine plantation, trees standing in rows like a marching band, studded the shoulder along much of its length. Deciduous trees mixed in at its base. Several culverts conveyed water beneath the main trail, but unobtrusively. At times it was possible to imagine you were walking through a remote (if manicured) forest.

A sign posted by the Conservation District said an old two track entering the preserve from the south was the remnant of one of the first carriage roads leading to Traverse City. That was difficult to absorb, given the lack of deep ruts after more than 150 years of European settlement.

As I explored the little preserve, my incredulity grew. To the east was a strip of repair garages, storage buildings, and a monster lot full of hundreds of trucking vans. To the west a hiking trail came out into the open behind a Home Depot box store and stormwater pit. How had the preserve escaped the developer's scalpel?

I pieced together the history as well as I could. One slab of the preserve was turned over to the township by the owners of the apartment complex in which I lived as compensation for the development of land. Developers of a mall to the north of the preserve had turned another portion over to the township. I am grateful for the laws and regulations that promote public benefit in exchange for the permission to develop open space. Here in the heart of impervious suburbia, a refuge—not wild but with elements of the wild—survived.

The first summer in which I lived beside the preserve, its surprising diversity of wildlife seemed to come out to greet me. A barred owl, porcupine, snapping turtle, and puff-nosed adder revealed themselves. Of course, deer, squirrels, and chipmunks dashed about in the woods as well. A great blue heron appeared once in a great while to dine at the wetland food bar.

It was harder to find out anything about Miller Creek, other than its placement in the watershed. It rises less than two miles from my home, traveling through a culvert under US-31 before twisting through the preserve, then emptying into the Boardman River less than a mile to the east of my apartment. There was scarcely a hit on the internet, some of them relating to the one-time mill on Kids Creek.

I learned the preserve and the creek by sight, sound, and feel. The red pines, at the height of summer, provided a cool shade, and just as in winter, purred when winds raced high in the canopy. In other areas of the preserve, water was dominant—not mighty water, but unassuming water. It sometimes hurtled around bends after storms, but in dry spells crept stealthily. It was fed by a slow-moving sheet of water passing through the wetlands. Always, if you stopped long enough, even with audible traffic noise reverberating off the pavement to the north, you heard the calming, low voice of the water.

One of the smaller tributary brooks hugged the base of the small bluff on which my apartment building sat. One summer night, unable to sleep, I walked out on my balcony for a glimpse of stars. A few beamed or flickered through the lights of the city to the north. Suddenly I heard the brook, quietly insistent on my attention, offering itself for consolation.

I stood there, unmoving, for many minutes. As I listened to the water a thrill traveled down my back. Trying to encase it in words that do not do it justice, I say something wild in me marveled at this undaunted little stream, coursing through a small slice of unmarred country, ever alive. It was in me, and I in it. The miracle of life has rarely embraced me in its tender arms as it did that night.

A Piece of the Soul

The year 1997 was a milestone in my career. Fifteen years in, I was disillusioned and defeated as never before. An environmental lobbyist, I was constantly exposed to the political process.

I hit a spiritual wall. At a time of accelerating environmental decline, the political system was mashing the gas pedal with sadistic glee.

The work, which had inspired me with a sense of possibility for a decade and a half, now inspired a sense of gathering crisis. Like a crumbling human relationship, my link to my job had frayed. I no longer loved it.

This was about the time a lobbyist fighting clean air standards proposed by the EPA brushed aside the argument they were needed to protect children suffering from asthma, saying, "Asthmatic kids need not go out and ride their bicycles." Another argued that EPA's cost–benefit analysis was rigged in favor of more rules because it treated the value of an older person's life—which is going to end soon anyway—the same as that of a younger person. The 1990s were a decade in which one political party tried to gut the Clean Water Act, terminated chemical industry fees that supported the Superfund toxic waste cleanup program, and enacted a policy that permitted contamination to remain in Michigan's groundwater instead of being cleaned up.

A colleague of mine indicated she never wanted to testify in front of state legislators on an environmental issue again. "Every time I go over to the capitol," she said, "it takes a piece out of my soul."

I knew what she meant. I had become a target of mild legislator abuse at some hearings. After testifying against an "agricultural disparagement" bill that proposed a food libel law against people who dared question the safety of the food supply, one lawmaker likened me to a watermelon. "Green on the outside, pink on the inside." My face flushed. I have ever since wished I had the presence of mind to say, "Sir, I am red, white, and blue all the way through."*

"Environment" is a word with an assortment of meanings. In the jargon of everyday press coverage, it was generally attached to an apparently narrow set of issues that rarely affects individuals immediately—air and water pollution, or the consumption of open space and sensitive lands.

But "environment" also means the place in which one lives or works—essentially, one's habitat. As an employee of a capitol-based nonprofit environmental coalition, I worked in an environment which, as the twentieth century ended, invited the question of how far into the twenty-first century we would last. The capitol was a fantasy land in which lies were truth, the corporate interest was the public interest, and those charged by the people with defending the environment were systematically pillaging it. The political process that defines Lansing and Washington showed warning signs of terminal illness. If anything, that process has accelerated since 1997.

And that, in turn, raises the issue of whether some of us who care about the environment are plagued by a disease. To continue—to persist—required that I examine my conscience and consider, whether as individuals or as a collective, we have time to heal the Earth.

Working within the political process necessarily clouds one's vision. Spawned by a public outcry in the early 1970s, the modern environmental movement grew organically from communities up, rather than from the capitol down. By the 1990s, the greatest successes and environmental energy animated activists at home, not politicians in their chambers. But distant politicians can either provide a foundation of support for citizen activism or snatch it away. In Lansing as well as Washington, they were hacking away at that foundation.

The policy defeats had been numerous and dangerous the previous few years. Michigan's former national leadership on environmental matters had been mocked

---

* The legislator was suggesting I was a "pinko"—communist.

by a succession of changes—everything from a law sticking taxpayers instead of companies with the bill for their pollution, to a secrecy law that gave corporations legal privilege to conceal some of their pollution, the same right to withhold information that was once afforded to husband and wife, physicians and patients, and attorneys and clients.

But there was more. Something coarse and ugly had entered the debate. Instead of admitting they favored repealing environmental laws, politicians and their corporate sponsors cloaked their daggers in the rhetoric of environmentalism. Instead of differing philosophically and openly with the arguments of environmental organizations—and many other public interest groups—the power elite attacked motives, denied facts, and huffed out a smokescreen of conservation sentiment.

My reaction was anger and outrage. Furious at the betrayal of our heritage, and indignant about the deception employed by our political leaders to consummate that betrayal, I found myself condemning and denouncing. Watching public servants who thought they were public masters belittle citizens who drove hundreds of miles and waited hours to speak for five minutes in defense of the environment, I clenched my fists and felt the adrenaline run.

But isn't the lesson of ecology that everything is interconnected? Can environmentalists heal anything if they employ the language, and embrace the ideology, of warfare? These questions still vex me, almost as much as the runaway pace of global environmental degradation that our system seems powerless to stop.

Knowing that I could not separate myself from what I hoped to accomplish, that I must live by the standards I demand in our civil society, I had to return to first principles. But even more, I needed to turn to my heart.

"Until he extends the circle of his compassion to all living things, man will not himself find peace," Albert Schweitzer said. And I realized that until I tried to understand with compassion why individual humans—including myself—and the human collective fail to come to grips with the environmental crisis of our times, I would get nowhere.

Before becoming a professional environmental advocate—I dreamed of revolution. Not a war of armies conducted to the hellish rhythm of gunfire, not even the domination of one person or point of view by another. I dreamed rather of an individual revolution, the revolution from within.

My readings and my life to that point taught that the most powerful lessons are neither legislated nor enforced at the tip of a bayonet but won through the suffering and growth of the human spirit. The growth, in turn, can lead to a startling revelation. There is no end to the majesty of the natural world and to the possibilities of the human creature, and in the end, to the healing power of love.

It was easy to stray from that dream. Again, if the lesson of ecology is that everything is interconnected, then it was almost impossible to separate myself from the climate in which I worked. As legislators repealed environmental protection while professing their love for clean air and water, I became cynical. Soon I nearly lost my ability to imagine that things could be better. But they can, and I desperately clung to the belief that they soon would.

Signs of hope were and are abundant, if I will only look. On the political front, I can find solace in polls that show whopping majorities of the American public favor stronger environmental policies. And some of the existing policies have redeemed their promise; air and water pollution are not as grave as they would have been.

But even more, I take heart from the rebound of spirituality. As more citizens of our nation and others turn to private or collective faiths, and to a belief in something surpassing material existence, I see emerging evidence of the revolution of which I once dreamed.

Are restless Americans coming home at last as the frontier finally disappears? In *The Practice of the Wild*, Gary Snyder quotes a Crow elder: "You know, I think if people stay somewhere long enough—even white people—the spirits will begin to speak to them. It's the power of the spirits coming up from the land. The spirits and the old powers aren't lost, they just need people to be around long enough and the spirits will begin to influence them."

I decided an environmentalism—a way of life—built on connection rather than domination, on understanding rather than warring, might in fact be possible. Wandering a patch of state-owned land not far from where I lived, I absorbed the wonder of the tender sky above and the strength of the Earth under my feet, and I mused—I felt—that the revolution is coming, just far more gradually than I once expected.

How did that help me when I returned to the political process? Did I murmur sweet words of peace to legislators? No, but I began to understand a little. Is it so difficult to fathom why in a time when our home, our Earth, is screaming from the wounds inflicted on it, that we are screaming at each other? Is it so difficult to understand why, in a culture still addicted to materialism that cannot fulfill us, our leaders crave more and more of the drug that provides a dwindling high? I suspect there is as much unconscious grief as conscious fury in the bitterness of some legislators fighting environmental protection.

And most importantly, having grown old enough to recognize my own frailties and flaws, my own mistreatment of fellow humans and the natural world, I found it was not so difficult to understand the wounds inflicted by others. I had more growing to do than I ever realized. The actions of those I challenged were different in degree, not in kind, from my own. There's no escaping it; we're all in this together. But I cannot gloss over the simple fact: there will be plenty of pain and division on the way to restoration of a safe and healthful global environment.

While we cannot afford to practice the equivalent of warfare or even think in its language, those who care about the environment will make enemies. The most peaceful among us will arouse fierce opposition. Our challenge is not to shun conflict but to face it with full awareness, humility, unflinching determination, and compassion for those taking the opposite view.

A generation of citizens and leaders in the 1960s and 1970s, for all their mistakes, had the guts and the foresight to take the first steps down the road toward environmental healing. Brushing aside the objections of many of the powerful and mighty, they responded to the pollution crisis by clamoring for and passing environmental laws. They set a standard for us.

The crisis we faced in 1997 and today is more fundamental, graver. We'll be remembered by how we respond in the next several decades.

Knowing that the laws we impose on ourselves, to which we willingly submit, are ultimately far more meaningful than the impermanent imperfect compromise creations of any legislature, I drew sustenance from a secular faith expressed in Michigan's 1963 Constitution. It is a starting point as good as any:

> Article 4, Section 52. The conservation and development of the natural resources
> of the state are hereby declared to be of paramount public concern in the interest
> of the health, safety and general welfare of the people.

In 1997, I decided to give the work of environmental protection renewed commitment, and it has carried me into the 2020s. Guided by the North Star of faith in the ultimate goodness of human beings and by the light of our souls and spirit, I still believe we can heal—we *will* heal—the Earth, and in so doing, ourselves.

Good Ancestors

I have had the privilege of meeting scores of the legends and heroes of Michigan's conservation and environmental movement. I met the vast majority in the Archives of Michigan, the University of Michigan Bentley Historical Library, and community libraries across Michigan.

I met them because I was researching matters for my first book, a history of Michigan conservation from the 1830s to the year 2000. Ushered by the guardians of community and state history to quiet areas where they brought the documents I had requested, I was already in a reverent mood before I looked at a single piece of paper. Opening the file folders and touching the documents sent chills down my spine. I was holding testimony from people long dead, who had thought about us.

I held a petition to the governor from citizens concerned about depleted fish stocks—a missive dating back to the 1870s. I uncovered a file of papers detailing the work of a modest Grand Rapids banker named Charles Garfield who from the 1880s to the 1920s, as a volunteer, championed the building of a state forest system from the ruins of the clear-cut, burned-over timber country of northern Michigan. I learned about one of the most unusual characters in Michigan political history, Governor Chase Osborn, who was among the early professional state game wardens in the late 1800s. (Michigan was the first state to establish such a professional force.)

Edith Munger joined the parade, working to educate Michiganders, especially children, about the beauty and value of the state's many bird species from 1910 to 1930.

These people and others devoted themselves to a mission whose fruits they would barely begin to see in their lifetimes. The solemn debt we owe them struck me as a revelation.

The night before I was to interview three modern-day pioneers, I sat in a Grayling motel reading *Timber*, by Harold Titus. Although not highbrow literature, it was an earnest novel about the battle to turn Michigan's forest from private plunder to public estate, benefiting multiple generations. As I lay in bed thinking that night, my eyes blurred with tears. Some of these long-gone conservationists described their cause in the language of dollars and cents, of practicality, of good public policy, and would have been embarrassed or annoyed had someone described their motivation as love—but love it was. Love of Michigan, its people, and its posterity. They had been thinking of me, and of my nearly 10 million fellow Michigan citizens. Their good works came all the way down over the decades, like the light shining from a faraway star that takes years to reach our eyes.

The next day began with a morning shot of whiskey and neared its end with two glasses of white wine. My first stop was the home of Merrill "Pete" Petoskey, a retired wildlife expert and manager who had served in both the Michigan Department of Natural Resources and the U.S. Forest Service. Born in 1923, he had served in the military like so many of his generation who later devoted their careers to conservation. Pete could be heard a mile away, bellowing because, it was said, his time with the field artillery of the U.S. Army during World War II had impaired his hearing.

Pete was part of a generation tempered by war. In the late 1960s and 1970s, most of the DNR's leaders were World War II vets whose work won Michigan national recognition. As longtime Michigan conservationist Tom Bailey wrote, "I had quite a few opportunities to observe these amazing men, and believe that a key factor in their generation's remarkable leadership is the fact that their schooling in both leadership and following took place for many of them literally under fire in the foxholes, ships, tanks and planes of World War II."[*]

Pete was on my interview list primarily because he had led a monumental effort to restore Michigan's deer hunting tradition. That tradition, for well over one hundred years, has been so important in northern Michigan communities that the

---

[*] Tom Bailey, *A North Country Almanac: Reflections of an Old-School Conservationist in a Modern World* (East Lansing: Michigan University Press, 2018).

first day of firearm deer season, November 15, is a school holiday. The Michigan Legislature calls off business that day as a custom.

When Pete came upon the scene, hunters grumbled even more than usual about the inadequate deer population. There was more demand than supply, hunters said; they always say that, but the official state deer count backed them up.

Believing that "there's more to hunting than a chunk of meat," Pete changed the name of his division from "Game" to "Wildlife Division." He vowed that the unsatisfactory state deer population would rebound to one million by 1980. His proposal to set aside $1.50 from every deer hunting license to fund deer management soon burgeoned to over $1 million in revenue annually. Thanks in large part to the policies he championed, the deer population exceeded a million before 1980. In the book for which I was interviewing him, I said Pete "is typical of a breed of wildlife professionals unafraid to challenge both established doctrine and the beliefs of his paying constituency, the hunters. Proud of their training and knowledge, committed to letting biology rather than politics govern their decisions, Petoskey and peers won a national reputation for Michigan as a wildlife leader."[†]

I approached the front door of his house near Lewiston that fall morning cautiously. I did not know Pete well, and it's not easy for me to get comfortable with people known for their outspokenness and critical judgment. Pete's reputation was of a man who spoke his mind, even when it cost him politically. I worried he would dismiss me as an environmental dilettante. I needn't have worried. Perhaps at age seventy-six he had mellowed, or perhaps I was simply wrong about his feelings about environmentalists. I would find he was dead serious about conservation but equipped with a sly sense of humor.

He greeted me warmly and asked whether I was hungry. He said he was preparing scrambled eggs and bacon. A vegetarian at the time, I said nothing about my aversion to meat, and thanked him for the offer. He led me inside and pointed to a chair at the kitchen table, a convenient anchoring point while he prepared breakfast.

"So, how's your research going?" he barked.

I told him I was pleased with my progress. I had the 1800s and first two decades of the twentieth century down pat, but I needed to plug some holes in the narrative after that. "Including a lot of the hunting and fishing history."

---

† The rebound of Michigan's deer population was not without its critics. Environmental advocates lamented the voracious eating capacity of deer, and attacked the Department of Conservation and later the Department of Natural Resources for "managing for deer"—for example, continuously planting aspen for deer food, preventing the natural succession of forestlands.

"Do you hunt or fish?" he said over his shoulder, not turning around to face me.

"Not really," I told him. "I've been out with hunters and fishermen to see what it's like. If I was going to write about these issues, I thought I'd have to at least observe."

"So the answer is no."

Embarrassed, I admitted it was.

I must have said this in a sheepish tone because he turned around and laughed uproariously. "It's not a sin, you know. Just asking." I relaxed, and the interview over breakfast went well. He had much to say about the game-to-wildlife transition during his career. He was glad of it but wanted to be sure I did not misrepresent him as a greenie. "The biology is and always has been what I based my decisions on, and what every fish and wildlife manager should. I can see where environmentalists are coming from—and a lot of the time they're wrong. You can't manage deer as if they're Bambi. That's emotion, and it's just plain foolish."

I asked him whether he thought there was a place at all for emotion in conservation and environmental policy debates. After all, wasn't the mission of saving the Earth something as primal as saving your family?

"Yeah, there's plenty of room for that. And I've seen every damn emotion you can name at our public hearings. Hunters can get upset about shortening a hunting season by a couple of days, same with the fishermen. Something tangible. Excuse me for saying this, but your environmentalist friends have crocodile tears for things that don't matter biologically."

When the interview was done, I put down my notepad and looked him in the eye. "I think it's time to drink a toast," I said. He looked surprised for only an instant before getting up to walk to a cupboard. Reaching up, he fetched a half-empty fifth of whisky and two shot glasses. He placed all three on the kitchen table. I poured the shot glasses full.

"Here's to the work you did that will pay off for Michigan, the sportsmen, the people for a long time to come." Hoping I didn't sound pompous, I said, "On their behalf, I thank you." We downed the shots. I thought his eyes glistened for a moment. He smiled.

After a few minutes of chatter, I excused myself. It was time to visit two more legends. "Sorry you gotta go," Pete hollered. "'Preciate your visit."

As we walked to the door, I said to him, "It's been an honor to spend the time with you."

Perhaps I had gushed too much, for he nodded and said nothing. I started my car and looked to the door. He was standing, watching me. I waved. After a beat, he waved, and then smiled.

Thinking it likely I would never see him again, I felt a thickness in my chest.

I was ahead of schedule, it turned out. The whisky must have dazed me. I was due in Frankfort at 4 and it was only 11. The drive would take ninety minutes. Then it came to me—I could stop at Hartwick Pines State Park on my way. The idea seemed inspired.

Hartwick Pines contains one of the few stands of old-growth Michigan white pine that survived the onslaught of the timber industry in the late nineteenth and early twentieth centuries. A popular walking trail winds through forty-nine acres of pine, some trees dating back four hundred years. I was in the mood for that.

I knew from my research that the stand of white pine existed because Karen Hartwick, the daughter of a lumber company co-founder, purchased it and another 8,000 acres from the Salling-Hanson company. She donated it to the state on the condition that the park be named after her husband, Edward Hartwick, who had died from spinal meningitis while stationed in France during World War I.

The early morning's overcast had yielded just enough to permit the sun occasionally to edge out a cloud and cast a wan shadow. But in the forty-nine-acre grove of memory—the memory of a time when white pine spread over vast reaches of the state, the northern two-thirds of the Lower Peninsula and most of the Upper Peninsula—the sun did not reach. The air was still and solemn. On this school day in October, only a few visitors trod the path.

Three years before my visit, the tree that was perhaps the most famous in Michigan had died here. A 1992 storm ripped the Monarch's crown, and the tree perished in 1996. One hundred fifty feet tall, it had had a circumference of twelve feet. Its age was estimated at 325 years.

I had never visited a redwood grove then, but I knew white pine, enormous for this part of the continent, did not compare with the height of the West Coast giants. Yet as I strolled through the grove that didn't matter. I imagined something incomparable—the trees, like the elders among us, telling a story of ages. Celebrating what was, warning us what we had become and could become, and attempting to convey their wisdom.

After an hour of wonder I returned to my car and drove to Grayling. I called my hosts to ask whether I could show up at 2:30 instead of four. Joan Wolfe said I would be welcome.

The last moments of the drive to Frankfort, after the road crested a hill, displayed a panorama of Lake Michigan a mile away and below. It was impossible not to feel a shiver of awe. Like the white pine, the lake was of a scale almost larger than a modern mind, penned in by daily demands, could grasp.

Before reaching the base of the hill I turned right, drove a quarter mile, and turned right again into a driveway leading up to an attractive house whose lawn was studded with bird feeders. Before I could exit the car, the side door of the house opened. Joan and Will Wolfe greeted me with smiles. I knew this would be a good visit.

Then in their early 70s, Joan and Will had been two of the leaders in the environmental movement that surged into local and state policymaking, beginning in the mid-1960s. As industrial pollution peaked and pesticides led to notorious bird kills, citizens in Michigan, as elsewhere, began to push back. Forcefully. And in the case of Joan and Will, effectively. Far from hippies, they were an upper middle-class couple, respected in their community, quick studies in how citizens could effectively influence decision-makers, persistent and, quietly, fierce as hell.

They were retired now but had a keen interest in environmental policy. We sat exchanging news and gossip about the unfortunate state of that policy under Governor Engler, which inspired them to tell stories about the days when they had been most active. Something had changed in the way government responded to public activism, Joan thought, but perhaps something had changed in the citizenry. She questioned whether concerned citizens cut checks to environmental groups and left the hard work to their professional staff. Not for the first time, I heard veterans of the movement speculate whether its professionalization had resulted in significant bad along with the good.

About an hour after I arrived, Will brought out the white wine. Like it, conversation flowed freely. They told story after story, memories of teaming with then Governor Milliken to enact the state's Environmental Protection Act in 1970, outflanking the crude anti-environmental State Senator Joe Mack to win legislative passage of the Inland Lakes and Streams Act of 1972. But I wanted to take them back to 1966, when Joan had started the organizing that led to the founding of the West Michigan Environmental Action Council (WMEAC), the state's first major environmental advocacy organization. As she told the story, I reflected on what had transpired over the next thirty-three years. All that early progress—and then a stalemate, when environmentalists and polluters locked horns, each inching ahead now and then before retreating.

When I asked for their thoughts about why that had happened, they said they didn't know, but offered their individual opinions. Politicians had become shameless—impossible to embarrass into doing the right thing; the economy had changed such that both husbands and wives were in the work force, reducing volunteer time; the issues had grown more complex, once visible pollution and destructive land use had been alleviated; business lobbies had gotten craftier by adopting the rhetoric of a clean environment while thwarting the proposals to bring it about.

Still, both had hope. They spoke of attitudes and obstacles that had stood in the way up until the mid-1960s. An event or trend could light a match and start a fire at any time.

After the wine, Joan and Will served a satisfying dinner as our talk continued. The conversation went late into the evening. I asked how they had gotten their start in conservation. Joan had grown up in Highland Park with parents who contributed considerable time to community affairs. Will had no family tradition of community activism but had become an active fly fisherman. In his childhood living on the Detroit River at Grosse Ile just before World War II, he had seen "tremendous weed growth" and stayed out of the polluted water but hadn't then made broader observations about the condition of the outdoors. He was delighted to find trout in the Rogue River, which wound through the Rockford area, when the Wolfes moved there in the late 1950s. But the same stream was also fouled by effluent from the Wolverine Tannery and a paper mill. "There was no outcry," Will said. "It was still too close to the Depression. The problem was too close to the bread and butter of the community."

They recalled neighbor Art Williams. "He was the first hands-on conservationist we'd ever met," Will said. Soon both of the Wolfes became activists in their own right. In the early 1960s, Joan became president of the Grand Rapids Audubon Club, trying to rally Audubon members to deal with the issues of habitat loss and pesticide use.

Joan was emphatic about one thing that evening—her style of advocacy and that of WMEAC was not confrontational. If it had been, she said, many of the allies WMEAC enlisted, such as church groups, PTAs and others, would never have joined forces. And Grand Rapids business leaders would not have backed WMEAC financially. The Wolfes became what they called "reluctant feminists," spurred by sexist treatment of Joan. When she became the first female chair of the state Natural Resources Commission in 1977, the departing chair half-jokingly said that Joan had "come aboard with all the traits of a normal female, not the least of which was a desire to be heard—frequently and with gusto!" He added, "Joan has good looks, personality, charm and all the other attributes we admire—but beyond that, she has the intellect and dedication so necessary in this work." Even the compliments were leavened with patronizing rhetoric.

It was past 10 o'clock when our conversation ended. The Wolfes had invited me to stay overnight when we arranged the trip, and I was glad to accept the invitation. Will showed me to a guest room upstairs and promised a large breakfast. I thanked him for the hospitality.

It was difficult to fall asleep. I thought back on the events of that day, seeing clearly a common denominator. I had been in the presence of giants, all of whom had told variations of the same story: think of the future—not only think, but act. In the words of Jonas Salk, "Our greatest responsibility is to be good ancestors." I had clinked glasses with three people who were indisputably among Michigan's good ancestors.

Fitz

T he first thing I have to say about this cherished companion is that his name was not Fritz. Many people got it wrong. He was Irish, not German, named after the favorite writer of my youth, F. Scott Fitzgerald.

Fitz came into my life two months after he was born in 2012. He had turned up on a breeder's web site, a tiny puppy dwarfed in his photo by a water bottle. The breeder's starter name for him was Pumpkin. He looked strong-willed from the start. In the photo his eyes conveyed determined rebellion.

Two of his physical quirks were outsized ears. They sprouted from his head like pinned-on Halloween accoutrements. One ear typically stood up while the other folded. Maybe it was this look that induced two different women picking up their kids at the neighborhood school to pull over in the falling snow one week to remark on his cuteness and inquire somewhat accusingly why I hadn't dressed him in a sweater. "You can buy them on Amazon, you know," said one. What they couldn't know was that Fitz embraced the cold. He enjoyed any temperature between fifteen and fifty-five. Above that, he suffered. A warm sun in March could tax him.

When he was three, he accompanied me on a move from Minnesota to Michigan. We got life down to a rhythm: up at 6, go for a half hour walk along the beach or at the nature preserve three miles away, then back home to consume breakfast.

After finishing his, Fitz would watch each movement of my hand to mouth until I finally dropped him a crumb.

Not long after we retrieved Fitz, a friend and I were talking about the succession of dogs we've known; suddenly the thought that Fitz, too, would be gone slammed into me with near-lethal force. My fierce, quirky canine was not immortal. It's the moment that arrives for anyone with a companion animal. I couldn't bear the thought.

Loyalty is one of a dog's most commented-upon virtues. Having been through three moves, a job change, and health issues in recent years, I counted on him. We were friends, loyal as two of different species can be.

And yet, in the end, dogs harbor a piece of wild. They submit to our commands but not always with great joy. They eat our food but they would eat three times as much if it were put before them. They enjoy playing with us, but I suspect many of them would sometimes rather join a pack of their own. We are not the end-all and be-all of Creation.

And if I ever doubted the wild in Fitz, that was dispelled every so often when, in the middle of the night, he emitted a blood-curdling howl that spans millennia of dog nature, and seemed to free him to romp with his fellows in a dream born of ages.

Coda

Bill McKibben's *The End of Nature* stirred significant controversy and great praise when it appeared in 1989. Even before reading it, I was moved by it. The title appealed to my sense of melodrama. The end of nature? Depressing beyond words. We were entering the epoch of post-nature.

Of course, the book's thesis is more complicated, and less depressing, than that. McKibben hasn't exactly been paralyzed by gloom and doom. For over three decades he has been a leading voice and conscience in the global fight against runaway climate change. The end of nature does not mean the end of conservation.

The twenty-five-year-old me who began work at the Michigan Environmental Council would have spent some time brooding over the idea that there were no "pristine" places left on Earth. But the sixty-four-year-old me who writes this would like to tell the MEC lobbyist not to waste his time on such sentiment, any more than he should waste time mourning the fact that Santa Claus does not exist. Part of the process of maturing is giving up childish things. A belief in "pristine" in the material world is one of them.

Humankind and the world we inhabit have always interacted. The scale of our effect on nature has grown enormously, but we cannot escape what we call nature's laws. We understand the universe better than we ever have, but there are unfathomable depths of discovery yet to plumb. We use science and experience to steward the environment but are frequently surprised by unforeseen consequences of our actions. We are fallible. We are mortal.

In his oft-quoted poem "The Peace of Wild Places," Wendell Berry speaks of despairing for the world in the night and going out and lying down "where the wood drake rests in his beauty on the water, and the great heron feeds. I come into the peace of wild things who do not tax their lives with forethought of grief." Does this use of "wild" imply that its definition is to thrive in the moment, unconscious of death? It is a rare moment when I have known that kind of wildness.

Is the distinction between the wild and the not-wild a false dichotomy? There is no wilderness and not-wilderness. There are no bright lines between the human animal and other animals, a dominion over Creation. All of life runs on a continuum of relationships.

Isn't it more accurate to say that humans now influence almost every process of the world, but cannot control a vast proportion of it?

I return to the comfort of my dog companions when I measure the boundary between wild and domestic. No matter how many centuries canines flourish under the hand of man, they will never completely shed their wildness. They will cry mournfully in their sleep, chase their tails, eat grass, wag their tails, snap at anyone with the chutzpah to reach for the bones in their mouth.

No matter how many centuries pass, no matter how much knowledge we glean and retain, humans will still be roiled by anger and electrified by joy, attracted to one another for reasons we cannot even express—and moved beyond measure by the rhythms and mysteries of the world outside.

The complex world and the elusive nature to which we belong are worth loving and fighting for.

Acknowledgments

utting a long environmental journey into perspective in this book brings up a multitude of faces and names who, at cost to themselves, have helped me make the voyage. I can't possibly thank them all. But here are a few who have had a particularly pivotal role: Patricia Widmayer, who for some reason helped land me a front-row seat for environmental policy on the governor's staff. Kathy Aterno of Clean Water Action, who picked me up off the floor and hired me in 1991. Carol Misseldine of the Michigan Environmental Council, who gave me a job at MEC in 1994. Lana Pollack, who supported me steadfastly at MEC after Carol's departure and gave me a chance to work binationally at the International Joint Commission. And Jim Olson and Liz Kirkwood, who gave me a home at FLOW (For Love of Water) as land came into sight. Each of these colleagues, supervisors, and mentors deserve thanks beyond what I can express here.

Thanks also to my brothers Jack and Tom, who have also picked me up off the floor more than once.

And thanks finally to Catherine Cocks, assistant director and editor-in-chief at Michigan State University Press, who gave the manuscript a chance.